What people are saying about Steve Kursh's

Minding the Corporate Checkbook

"I agree strongly with the author that Return on Investment (ROI) is not by itself a sufficient justification for most of today's business investments, particularly those that involve a large amount of 'gut-based' emotional decisions. This book provides a defensible, repeatable, and transferable decision-making process that will help the reader become more effective when spending his company's money."

—Michael Hoch, Research Director,
Aberdeen Group

"This book does a great job laying out the importance of considering more than just the pure 'ROI numbers' of an investment, and forces you to think about the implementation and follow-up needed. It should be read by anyone who has the opportunity or ability to change the way capital is invested."

—Jim Connelly, Regional Vice President of Finance,
Mariott International, Inc.

"*Minding the Corporate Checkbook* reaffirms the notion that business value is brought about by successful execution and continued supervision, and not solely determined by preliminary due diligence. The scope of this book is applicable to internal corporate endeavors, as well as a variety of other investments. After reading this book, I find myself applying these execution and post-investment management techniques to a variety of my venture capital deals, as well as better assessing new investment opportunities through more pragmatic exit strategy evaluations."

—Rudolph J. Morando Jr., Associate,
Rex Capital Advisors, LLC

"This is a very lucidly written book that provides a new qualitative framework for business decision-making. The primary contribution is to provide a decision-maker with a process that can be used to complement existing (and often abused) financial-number-driven analysis. The author has provided a very helpful and effective resource for practitioners—both managers and consultants—and people who are regularly inundated by numbers but may not have the time to put these numbers in the context of a particular capital decision-making process."

—*Dr. Atreya Chakraborty, Senior Consultant,*
The Brattle Group

"Through consulting, I have witnessed far too many failed investments—and even worse, failing companies!—that could have been avoided by applying the lessons contained in this book. Anyone can read this book and apply the tools his type of investment analysis."

—*Jack Mazur, Senior Financial Consultant,*
Parson Consulting

"Projects too often fail not because the financial calculations were wrong, but because the execution and subsequent management were not considered carefully enough. Steve Kursh's new book makes a unique contribution by providing a framework that helps us better deal with both the execution phase of a project and its ongoing management."

—*Lal C. Chugh, Ph.D., Professor of Finance,*
University of Massachusetts

Minding the Corporate Checkbook

FT Prentice Hall

FINANCIAL TIMES

In an increasingly competitive world, it is quality
of thinking that gives an edge—an idea that opens new
doors, a technique that solves a problem, or an insight
that simply helps make sense of it all.

We work with leading authors in the various arenas
of business and finance to bring cutting-edge thinking
and best learning practice to a global market.

It is our goal to create world-class print publications
and electronic products that give readers
knowledge and understanding which can then be
applied, whether studying or at work.

To find out more about our business
products, you can visit us at www.ft-ph.com

Pearson
Education

Minding the Corporate Checkbook

A Manager's Guide to Executing Successful Business Investments

Steven R. Kursh

FINANCIAL TIMES
Prentice Hall

An Imprint of PEARSON EDUCATION

Upper Saddle River, NJ • New York • London • San Francisco • Toronto • Sydney
Tokyo • Singapore • Hong Kong • Cape Town • Madrid
Paris • Milan • Munich • Amsterdam

www.ft-ph.com

Library of Congress Cataloging-in-Publication Data

A CIP catalog record for this book can be obtained from the Library of Congress

Editorial/Production Supervision: Wil Mara
Cover Design Director: Jerry Votta
Cover Design: Talar Boorujy
Art Director: Gail Cocker-Bogusz
Manufacturing Manager: Alexis R. Heydt-Long
Acquisitions Editor: Jim Boyd
Marketing Manager: John Pierce

© 2004 Pearson Education, Inc.
Publishing as Financial Times Prentice Hall
Upper Saddle River, New Jersey 07458

Prentice Hall offers excellent discounts on this book when ordered in quantity for bulk purchases or special sales. For more information, please contact: U.S. Corporate and Government Sales, 1-800-382-3419, corpsales@pearsontechgroup.com. For sales outside of the U.S., please contact: International Sales, 1-317-581-3793, international@pearsontechgroup.com.

Printed in the United States of America

First Printing

ISBN 0-13-100288-0

Pearson Education Ltd.
Pearson Education Australia Pty., Limited
Pearson Education Singapore, Pte. Ltd.
Pearson Education North Asia Ltd.
Pearson Education Canada, Ltd.
Pearson Educación de Mexico, S.A. de C.V.
Pearson Education—Japan
Pearson Education Malaysia, Pte. Ltd.

FINANCIAL TIMES PRENTICE HALL BOOKS

For more information, please go to www.ft-ph.com

Business and Society

Douglas K. Smith
  On Value and Values: Thinking Differently About We in an Age of Me

Economics

David Dranove
  What's Your Life Worth? Health Care Rationing…Who Lives? Who Dies? Who Decides?

Entrepreneurship

Oren Fuerst and Uri Geiger
  From Concept to Wall Street: A Complete Guide to Entrepreneurship and Venture Capital

David Gladstone and Laura Gladstone
  Venture Capital Handbook: An Entrepreneur's Guide to Raising Venture Capital, Revised and Updated

Thomas K. McKnight
  Will It Fly? How to Know if Your New Business Idea Has Wings… Before You Take the Leap

Stephen Spinelli, Jr., Robert M. Rosenberg, and Sue Birley
  Franchising: Pathway to Wealth Creation

Executive Skills

Cyndi Maxey and Jill Bremer
  It's Your Move: Dealing Yourself the Best Cards in Life and Work

Finance

Aswath Damodaran
  The Dark Side of Valuation: Valuing Old Tech, New Tech, and New Economy Companies

Kenneth R. Ferris and Barbara S. Pécherot Petitt
  Valuation: Avoiding the Winner's Curse

International Business and Globalization

John C. Edmunds
  Brave New Wealthy World: Winning the Struggle for World Prosperity

Johny K. Johansson
  In Your Face: How American Marketing Excess Fuels Anti-Americanism

Peter Marber
  Money Changes Everything: How Global Prosperity Is Reshaping Our Needs, Values, and Lifestyles

Fernando Robles, Françoise Simon, and Jerry Haar
  Winning Strategies for the New Latin Markets

Contents

Appendix: Accounting and Finance: 205

Bibliography 235

Index 239

PREFACE

I have followed a long, circuitous route to this book, but the value of the journey has far exceeded the sum of the steps. Many years ago, as a founder of a software company, I faced the same challenge of most managers: Strategies seem so wonderful in theory, but how do you execute them in real time to grow corporate value? Concepts that I learned in graduate school and from best-selling business books seemed to make good sense, but rarely, if ever, could I implement them at my company.

After successfully exiting the company and returning to academia, I had time to reevaluate my own experience as a manager. I realized the sway given to an idea or set of strategies because of its apparent success at another company or companies. All too often, unfortunately, these "solutions of the day" take an enormous amount of resources and effort, but usually produce minimal growth in corporate value. It took me a while to realize it, but strategies are like shoes—few of us easily fill another person's shoes, regardless of the cliché to the contrary. Companies, like people, are unique, and there is no one right way or set of ways of doing business that always work, even within the same industry.

Business is not brain surgery. Most of what we need to do to succeed and to grow value at our companies is not fancy or special. Yet, the key to success in business is in identifying the *obvious* and in executing it well. Too many companies and their people, however, devote resources to grand strategies and ideas, instead of focusing on the boring basics of getting the job done. Clearly, the bubble years of the late nineties were an exemplification of too much talk by management and not enough action to grow revenue and profits.

It's my hope that you will find this book to be different from other books that you've consulted. My focus is on the processes that you follow to evaluate business investments, rather than on your specific strategies. In the pages that follow, you'll find tools, what I broadly label "The Business Investment Roadmap^{TM}," that enable you to execute your strategies to grow corporate value by making successful investments. Indeed, I believe firmly that most companies already have in place the resources and people to grow value without the necessity of major transformation efforts or the implementation of complicated new systems for measuring performance.

In business, there's a tremendous amount of "low-hanging fruit" that's ripe for the picking; before we worry about making strategic changes or getting involved with what some might call broad-based "happy talk of simple solutions," we can grow corporate value by improving our processes to "pick that fruit." It's not hard; the difficult part is having the discipline to implement better processes to make the strategies work to grow corporate value.

At varying times, I have worked as a college professor, a businessman, and a consultant. Much of what follows reflects what I have learned in my career. I owe a tremendous debt of gratitude to many people who have helped me in my career and provided me insights through their writings and in discussions. With the rare exception of geniuses who truly make the world a better place through original work, most of us can hope only to contribute by extrapolating from the work of others and our own experiences.

Several people had an instrumental role in making this book possible. The team at Financial Times, Prentice Hall has provided insight, support, and perspective throughout the entire process. Executive Editor Jim Boyd has constantly amazed me with the quality and timing of his responses. On many occasions, I sent him an email very late in the evening or during a weekend day and was surprised to find a return email from him shortly thereafter that was written even later that evening. Wil Mara, the Production Editor, was very helpful and responsive. Leah Johnson, the Field Editor, played an important role in getting me to consider writing a book with her company.

My colleagues at Northeastern University have helped me in many ways. I owe special thanks to Joe Meador, Coleen Pantalone, Harlan Platt, Jon Welch, Ira Weiss, and Roger Atherton who, along with other colleagues, enabled me to return to my true calling as a professor after I exited the software business. Several of my colleagues in the College of Engineering and the College of Business, including Paul Bolster and Jeff Born, have given me the opportunity to be an active member of the faculty in areas of interest to me. I still cannot believe that I get paid to work with such wonderful people, teach and learn from such delightful students, and spend time researching and learning about such interesting issues.

I've also benefited from discussions with and ideas from friends and family. Joel Shulman, a Professor at Babson College, took the time to read early drafts, and he provided innumerable contributions. Jon Buxton shared many ideas and discussions with me as the book proceeded. Saul Pannell was a sounding board for many of my ideas. Stew DeBruicker, formerly a Wharton School professor, inspired me to pursue a career in academia. My brother, Sam Kursh, a Director at LECG, has been a constant source of encouragement and knowledge throughout my career.

Many former students, clients, and colleagues also helped make this book possible. Lal Chugh from the University of Massachusetts, Jim Connelly from Marriott, Elizabeth Coveney from Coke, Chris Higgins from Booz, Allen & Hamilton, Michael Hoch from Aberdeen, Jack Mazur from Parsons Consulting, Anurag Mehndiratta from Siemens, Rudy Morando from Rex Capital, and Dennis Shaughnessy from Charles River Laboratories devoted the time and energy to review drafts of the book, providing great suggestions for improvements. James Donovan, a former graduate student, worked closely with me. I found his help invaluable, particularly with the execution of the Fresh Breeze company example, the appendix, and the chapter on risk. Speaking professionally, I know that I can trust him to get the job done within the iron triangle of budget, scope, and time. To all of these former students, clients and colleagues, I offer my gratitude; however, any faults within the material that follows are my own.

Finally and most importantly, I offer my heartfelt thanks to my wife and my children. Nan provided constant encouragement and support throughout the process of writing this book. She edited text, usually late at night, and she rarely complained about my absence from family life. My daughters, Eliza, Logan, and Hayden, visited me frequently at my office and entertained me with stories from their school days. Thank you all for your patience and your generous goodwill.

1

Investing Successfully for Your Future

"At the end of the day you get nothing for nothing."

Foreman in Les Misérables, *musical by Alain Boublil, Claud-Michel Schönberg, lyrics by Herbert Kretzner, original novel by Victor Hugo*

The Challenge We Face

It is the day after the day after. The party was great while it lasted, the hangover was painful and miserable, and the cleanup of the mess that companies made is nearly finished. Outrageous ideas for businesses no longer receive funding, and the previous decade's unfortunate combination of arrogance and youth in the business world is long gone. The basics are back in style, and talk of revolution is now a subject for history classes, not corporations.

Even the stock market has recovered. Although we are still far from the heights reached in early 2000, as early 2004, the NASDAQ was up over 85 percent from its lows in October 2002. The Dow Jones Industrial Average hit a five-year low in October 2002, but since then it has risen by more than a third. Unemployment is also falling, and there is at least limited optimism about the future for many companies.

The challenge now is investing a company's resources successfully for the future while remembering some of the financial hurt from the past. A quick survey of the business press finds stories detailing failed IT investments, failed mergers and acquisitions, failed human resource management initiatives, failed products and service offerings, and failed research and development efforts from the late 1990s to today. A consistent theme for all of these failures is loss: loss of shareholders' money; loss of time, energy, career growth opportunities, confidence, and even jobs for employees and managers; and loss of management will and desire to invest resources in their corporations' futures. Today, it seems that managers don't just keep an eye on expenses; they have glued their checkbooks shut.

At the same time, companies must grow revenues and profits to survive, let alone prosper. Growth in revenue and profits starts with investments in capital goods (e.g., machinery, equipment, and computers) and people (new employee hires and training for existing employees that increases their productivity). Avoiding investments in capital goods and human capital entirely and indefinitely might be an extremely short-sighted way to manage a company.

The advances in the values of many publicly traded stocks in 2003 and early 2004 indicated that the stock market expects future growth and profitability from such investments, which is reflected in rising stock prices. The key to meeting these expectations is growth in revenue and earnings, but without investments in capital goods and people this growth is not likely. Little will be gained without the critical ingredients of more equipment and people.

Data from the U.S. Department of Commerce indicates that many companies, both publicly traded and closely held, are not making investments for the future, or even attempting to improve efficiency today. Business capital spending fell from 11.8 percent in 2001 to 10.6 percent in 2002. Although data on spending for the last part of 2002 was very encouraging, anecdotal information, including surveys of executives, indicated that overall investment activity is likely to be sporadic and volatile, particularly when interest rates rise. Anecdotal evidence, including statements by business leaders that they are "still waiting" for capital spending to pick up and "don't see" the need to hire more employees, indicates that investment activity is likely to remain relatively low, particularly when compared to the late 1990s.

Yes, some companies, as reflected in recent government statistics, are beginning to invest, but these companies are the exception, not the rule. With the exception of a selected set of companies in a few economic sectors, companies are not investing in capital equipment and goods to enable greater efficiencies and growth. The decline involves much more than just technology-related investments; it is pervasive across nearly all types of capital goods and equipment.

Employment growth is similarly dismal. Whereas many of us once felt that we could leave our jobs and find something better relatively quickly, today most people are content to just have a job. Layoffs continue to loom, and even profitable companies are cutting back on employees. Indeed, many observers have taken to calling the current upswing in the economy a "jobless recovery."

You probably know someone (or are such a person yourself) who continues to get his or her old car fixed again and again rather than purchase a new one, no matter how cheap the financing terms offered by the automakers (zero-percent financing is about as cheap as you can get). Why does George Foreman, former heavyweight boxing champion and current spokesman for Meineke mufflers, tell us that he won't pay a lot for that muffler?

The reasons people offer for replacing exhaust systems and making other repairs to their old autos rather than letting the old cars die and buying new ones vary, but a key consideration for many people is a concern about the future, particularly after suffering the pain of a downturn in the economy. No one wants to waste their money while difficult economic times are still fresh in their minds. Nothing focuses the mind like fear, and the reminder of pain from recessions past is present in our thoughts.

Corporate decision makers apply the same logic to business investments—the hangover, long and painful, is still with us; it just seems to make sense to delay or avoid investments for growth and efficiency right now. The concern is survival, not growth. Finance departments at many companies seem to know only one word—*no*—in response to funding requests.

Return on Investment and Finance Metrics Are Not Enough

The hesitancy at corporations to invest in growth or greater efficiencies is particularly curious given that many of these prospective investments pass the traditional finance metrics of return on investment (ROI) with flying colors. Put simply, following traditional finance metrics, a company should invest when the expected return from an investment is greater than the costs incurred to make that investment. From a strictly theoretical perspective, it makes sense to invest when your returns are greater than the costs of the investment. Obviously, companies should select investments that both fit within strategic objectives and provide the greatest return relative to costs, but even with these caveats, the data on capital spending and human capital clearly indicate that companies are not doing much investment of any kind, even in investments with high ROIs.

Like a child who shouts louder in response to an initial "no" answer, many vendors have raised their voices regarding ROI and other finance metrics to support the purchase of their products and services. Some companies even have ROI calculators on their Web sites. Try one—it can be fun to pretend that you are making an investment. Plug in different numbers and—surprise!—the calculator will likely give you a high ROI value. Check out sales literature, too; many companies in a wide range of industries—human resources management services, credit cards, technology products and services—claim high ROIs and short payback periods (how quickly you will get the money you invest back in returns). Several companies claim almost immediate financial returns, implying that an investment in their product or service is nearly equivalent to free cash pouring into your business. Unfortunately for vendors and people looking for work, the shouts of "high ROI" still do not work; companies just are not investing or hiring. There is an economic recession in spending for capital goods, and an economic depression in the labor market.

The Paradox

There is a paradox here. Senior managers know that they must grow revenues and profits. They recognize that low revenue and profit growth could mean the loss of their own jobs. Mid-level managers are hesitant to propose new investment opportunities, and finance departments are applying greater levels of rigor to every corporate funding proposal. The exception is when senior management wants specific investments to be made. In these instances, no matter what the financial analysis shows, managers go along for political reasons and survival. Apart from these "pet" investments, it seems increasingly difficult to get resources for new investments that could result in greater revenue growth, efficiencies, and higher profits. A common maxim, "Nothing ventured, nothing gained," describes the situation well; in this case, very little is being ventured, so it should not be surprising when little is gained.

Visions and Strategies, Finance Metrics, and the Execution Gap

Broad visions and grand strategies are a wonder to behold. Who hasn't felt like they were making a difference in their company by helping to develop a "strategic plan"? You might have felt the excitement after participating in the presentation or viewing a PowerPoint presentation that outlines your company's strategy, often by providing examples of what "worked" for a different company at a different time. It seems so simple: All you need to do is adopt those best practices or the strategies identified at the winning companies, and your company, too, can achieve sustainable growth in revenues and profits that will create value for your shareholders. What's not to like?

The problem is that vision statements and strategies are broad, sweeping generalizations. They are important, but at best they provide only a framework and the starting point for creating shareholder value. At worst, they become the standard reference point that people in a company use to support and justify almost anything. In fact, sometimes it seems that vision statements and strategies are like horoscopes, always offering advice that is general enough to apply to everyone, but not specific enough for anyone to really act on the advice.

At the other extreme from vision statements and strategies, finance-based metrics, like ROI, provide a proven methodology for allocating scarce corporate resources. The methodologies of finance are straightforward and logical: gather the data, do the analysis, get the answers, and make the decision. The analysis and results can be easily replicated, and the facts are on paper. The facts resulting from financial analysis appear to be black and white, and, therefore, some people argue that financial analysis and ROI are the way to allocate corporate resources.

If you have sought corporate resources for an investment in new plant and equipment or personnel, you probably have experienced the process, sometimes painful and always time consuming, of building the business case for the investment. (A business case is essentially a financial model showing that the financial returns to the company will exceed the cost of the investment.) Outside of a general reference, broad strategies and visions have no standing in the development of a business case: it is numbers pure and simple. Still, the finance department can, and usually does, say no.

Unfortunately, finance metrics, the key variables in business cases, often do not mean much once the investment is made. Consider the Quaker acquisition of Snapple. The deal was easily justified by financial projections. Unfortunately for Quaker shareholders, the projections did not take into account the fact that Snapple did not fit into Quaker's business model, which was focused on the supermarket distribution channel, rather than Snapple's target channels of small retail stores, restaurants, and delicatessens. In less than two years, the value of Snapple declined by more than 75 percent, based on the price paid by buyout firm Thomas Lee & Partners. A short time later, after rebuilding the value Quaker had inadvertently destroyed, Thomas Lee & Partners sold Snapple to Pepsi for a sizable profit. From the perspective of Thomas Lee & Partners, it was a tremendous deal. Needless to say, for Quaker shareholders it was anything but a good deal, and many senior managers left Quaker. Quaker is now a division of Pepsi, largely as a consequence of the failed Snapple deal.

More recently, AOL Time-Warner decided to drop AOL from its name. This decision was obviously more than a name change; it acknowledged the failure of the merger between two very different companies that was supported by extensive financial analysis. The stock price of AOL Time-Warner has fallen more than 70 percent from the time of the merger and, as of late 2003, was not worth much compared with the value of Time-Warner itself prior to the merger. These numbers are particularly astonishing when you consider the accolades that AOL and Time Warner managers received from institutional investors (the people who manage pension fund money) and the business press at the time of the deal. Statements like "deal of the century" and "merger of the new economy and the old economy" were bandied about, and Ted Turner, the largest single shareholder in Time-Warner, compared his enthusiasm for the transaction to his anticipation of losing his virginity in his youth. The failure of this deal has already been and will continue to be fodder for numerous business books and business magazine articles.[1]

---

1. See, for example, Kara Swisher with Lisa Dickey, *There Must Be a Pony in Here Somewhere: The AOL Time-Warner Debacle and the Quest for the Digital Future* (New York: Crown Business, 2003).

A tremendous number of acquisitions fail to achieve their expected financial returns because management does not execute the investments within the overall context of their organizations, people, and strategies. They seem to ignore that the real issue is making the acquisitions work. The critical execution issues are related to the who, what, when, where, why, and how of the deal, particularly in relation to bridging the gap between the financial analysis and the grand statements made at the time of the deal.

The limits of financial metrics as decision tools are not just apparent with mergers and acquisitions. More often than not, information technology investments are supported by financial analysis framed in the context of the technology, rather than the more important and critical issues of how the investment will leverage the existing strengths and competitive advantages of the company. Consider the investments that many companies have made in customer relationship management (CRM) systems. Many of these CRM systems were implemented without sufficient input and participation by the primary users (the sales forces), a critical execution-related factor. Monster.com, for example, spent more than $1 million to acquire and implement CRM software. The resulting system was so slow and difficult to use that the Monster.com sales force simply stopped using it. Monster's experience is not a rarity. Many large banks have invested in CRM systems and received zero or only minimal returns, even excluding training time and costs for their staffs.

Even research and development (R&D) investments that are justified financially might not provide the expected returns to shareholders. Several researchers have found no relationship between a company's investment in R&D and positive returns to investors. Look at the returns to the respective shareholders of Dell Computer and Sun Microsystems as an example. As Figure 1.1

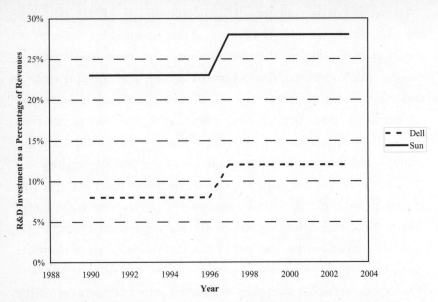

Figure 1.1   R&D Investment for Dell and Sun Corporations (as a Percentage
of Revenues)

indicates, Dell spends much less on R&D as a percentage of revenues than Sun Microsystems. In the past 10 years, however, Dell
shareholders have received more than 10 times the financial returns
of Sun's shareholders, reflected in the market capitalization of the
two companies, shown in Figure 1.2. A dollar invested in Dell in
the early 1990s would have returned to its investor more than 10
times the amount of a dollar invested in Sun. As of late fall 2003,
Sun was trading at less than $4.00 a share, significantly less than
its highs of a few years ago. One indicator of the company's difficult position is that it has reported a tenth consecutive quarter in
which revenues were lower than the comparable quarter for the
previous year. The stock market has apparently decided that Sun
has too far to go from its visions to the reality of growing revenue
and profits.

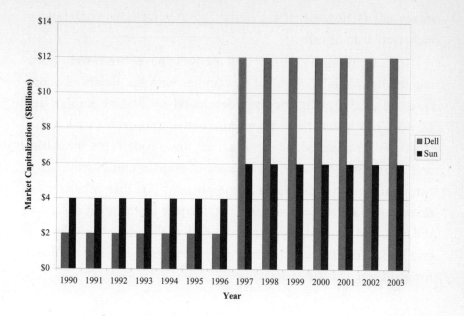

Figure 1.2   Market Capitalization for Dell and Sun Corporations

Dell spends significantly less on R&D as a percentage of revenue compared to Sun, but Dell has a much higher market capitalization. Although spending on R&D tells only part of the story of
the differences between Dell and Sun, there are many other examples that reinforce the point that investments in R&D do not necessarily result in increased company value. Consider IBM, which in
the late 1980s was investing more in R&D than the rest of the
computer industry combined. In fact, IBM's R&D spending was
eclipsed only by that of the federal government. At the same time,
the flow of products through IBM's pipeline was barely a trickle,
compared to other technology sector companies, and the company's market capitalization suffered as a consequence. By the late
1990s, IBM had cut its investment in R&D as a percentage of revenue by more than a third; at the same time, it substantially

increased its flow of new products, and returns to shareholders increased dramatically.

The limitations of financial analysis have been well documented by others. You might be familiar with the Balanced Scorecard, an analytical framework developed by Robert Kaplan and David Norton that provides an alternative approach to what they label the "traditional financial accounting model" for measuring and managing corporate performance.[2] Kaplan and Norton advocate that financial measures are important, but that other factors drive corporate success as well. As evidenced by the great success of the Balanced Scorecard in the marketplace, they are absolutely correct and, indeed, financial analysis is necessary but not sufficient for achieving corporate strategies.

The Execution Gap

There is a major gap between visionary strategies and financial analysis. At one extreme are the bold strategies of where we would like to be, and at the other extreme are finance-based analytical tools for evaluating investment opportunities that need to be made as an important step in reaching those strategic objectives. Unfortunately, neither the grand visionary strategies nor financial tools are enough on their own. There is a huge gap between strategy and financial analysis, what we call the *execution gap*. As shown in Figure 1.3, the execution gap is where managers create value for their companies by building a bridge between the financial analysis and corporate strategies. This step is *the essential task* and responsibility of management.

---

2. Robert S. Kaplan and David P. Norton, *The Balanced Scorecard* (Boston: Harvard Business School Press, 1996).

In one of his earliest meetings with security analysts after becoming IBM's CEO, Lou Gerstner, who recently retired from IBM, said that "the last thing IBM needs right now is a vision." Gerstner and his management team then committed their company to the business basics of execution. The company's subsequent success is well documented, and although Gerstner was obviously referring specifically to IBM when he made that statement more than 10 years ago, his words were prescient for all of us today.

Note the key word of *execution* as compared with the word *vision*. Gerstner clearly recognized the importance of getting the job done versus merely talking about it, and he focused the company's efforts accordingly. He was emphasizing the importance of moving away from management theories and talk to reality and results.

Gerstner's comments are not an isolated thought by an individual manager. The new CEO at General Electric, Jeff Immelt, was recently quoted in the *Wall Street Journal*. When discussing two major acquisitions by his company he said, "Most companies ultimately get judged on their ability to take a good strategy and execute it." Note again the key word *execution*.

In fact, the word *execution* is in the title of a recent best-selling business book, *Execution: The Discipline of Getting Things Done*.[3] The authors of that book, Larry Bossidy, the former CEO of Allied Signal (now Honeywell), and Ram Charan, a consultant with McKinsey, write, "Execution is the great unaddressed issue in the business world today. Its absence is the single biggest obstacle to success and the cause of most of the disappointments that are mistakenly attributed to other causes."

The fact that Lou Gerstner, the CEO of IBM, Jeff Immelt, the CEO of General Electric, and Larry Bossidy, the CEO of Honey-

---

3. Larry Bossidy and Ram Charan, *Execution: The Discipline of Getting Things Done* (New York: Crown Business, 2002).

well, are focused on execution indicates its importance in the executive suite and for senior-level managers. Execution is just as important for midlevel managers, those charged with the day-to-day task of getting the job done. Many midlevel managers are often caught between the extremes of expectations of achievement of strategic visions and the constraints of financial tools. You want to get the job done well, but the execution gap holds you and your company back.

Although measurement and management systems like the Balanced Scorecard can provide an alternative to bridging the execution gap, most companies and most managers within them do not have the time or resources to devote to the development or implementation of broad-based management initiatives. These initiatives can often be very useful, but those managers on the firing line every day frequently find that what works in the corporate classroom is often just too complicated or difficult to remember or keep track of in the battlefield of day-to-day business. It is hard enough just to catch up with the work that piled up while you were away at a corporate seminar and training program, let alone put what you have learned into practice. Besides, you might have had the experience of being burned by your manager, who simply ignores you when you try to implement what you have learned, often with a comment along the lines of, "That's nice, but we have got to get the job done now."

You might be familiar with *Good to Great* by Jim Collins, which is one of the most successful business books of the past decade.[4] Collins and his team studied companies in the Fortune 500 from 1965 through 1995 to determine which companies made, using their words, "the leap" from good to great. Their findings

---

4. Jim Collins, *Good to Great: Why Some Companies Make the Leap and Others Don't* (New York: HarperBusiness, 2001).

and suggestions for senior management are excellent, but, unfortunately, they are simply not enough in terms of the execution that is needed on a day-to-day basis by all levels of management to make the "leap." After reading books like *Good to Great,* you feel excited and enthusiastic about what should or could be done in your company, but ultimately you are left without a clear roadmap for implementing such fundamental changes.

This book provides you with a fabric that meshes the energy and the transformative capabilities of strategy together with the basic blocking and tackling of business basics, including basic and essential financial performance metrics. This approach does not require you or your company to go through extensive and expensive corporate transformation efforts. Read on, and you will see how you can build your existing methodologies and approaches to become significantly better and more effective at evaluating and executing the investments your company needs to gain efficiencies, grow your business, and increase your profits.

This approach enables you to move from theory and talk to reality and results, because it puts everyone in your company on the same page, allows them to see an investment through from the beginning to the end, helps to ensure that precious resources are not squandered, and provides opportunities to increase value for all stakeholders in your company. You will be able to leverage your existing knowledge and resources and get an immediate benefit in the work that you and your team are involved with every single day.

The key theme throughout the pages that follow is that success comes not from the choice of a specific investment, but from developing the competencies to assess and to manage the investments your company does choose with a clearly defined, disciplined approach, an approach called the Business Investment Roadmap™. Fundamentally, the Business Investment Roadmap is built on the concept that successful investments require a mastery of the business basics. If you are used to analyzing opportunities primarily with financial metrics, you will see that the Business Investment Roadmap uses financial analysis as only one (albeit important) aspect of the investment process, and, therefore, it complements and enhances traditional finance-based analytics, rather than substitutes for them.

The Business Investment Roadmap connects strategies to financial analysis; it gives you the framework to bridge the execution gap. In fact, although ROI and other finance-driven analytical tools will certainly remain important in evaluating investment opportunities, the most crucial metrics are those that will enable you to achieve and deliver the promised returns to your company's shareholders. These are execution-driven metrics, and they directly relate to the who, what, when, where, why, and how of investments.

The Business Investment Roadmap

This book focuses on what really matters: making and executing investments that grow the value of your company. Traditional approaches to investment analysis typically involve performing complex financial analysis primarily *before* an investment decision is made, rather than throughout the investment process. In addition, these approaches tend to be focused on execution only after the investment decision has already been made. One of the most important ways that the Business Investment Roadmap is different is that both execution and evaluation are important *before, during,* and *after* making an investment. With the Business Investment Roadmap, your assessment of investment opportunities begins by considering execution-related issues even before the detailed financial analyses. You will see that financial metrics are still quite relevant in your analysis of investments, but you must also think of returns in terms of risks and execution.

You will also be asked to evaluate investments that your company has already made. Historically, companies have devoted too much time and energy to analysis prior to making investments. Once investments have been started, however, they are often treated as if they are irrevocable. It is rare that companies devote sufficient resources to looking back and learning from past investments to improve the success of future investments. Some failures are much more dramatic than others, and some of the worst failures are investments that could have been stopped earlier, if someone had just taken the time and effort to reassess the investment after the initial decision was made and as conditions changed. For example, think about the investment of more than $1 billion made (and lost) by IBM in OS/2, an operating system that was supposed to compete with Microsoft Windows. At some point along the way, once Windows was clearly established in the marketplace, IBM should have pulled the plug. Most investments are not the equivalent of jumping off a cliff with no returns, but, rather, journeys that can be stopped along the way or changed when you run into detours along the road.

Using the Business Investment Roadmap, you will be able to develop and use methodologies that do the following:

1. Link your evaluation of investments directly to your company's strategies to grow value.

2. Improve your investment management competencies to minimize the risk of failures.

3. Enable you to evaluate past investments and determine the key factors for success in the future.

A Note of Caution

The Business Investment Roadmap, and the analytical framework behind the methodologies, will help you and your company make investments more effectively and efficiently, but they are not *the* single solution or set of strategies that will guarantee high returns to your stakeholders. Unfortunately, there is no miracle business solution or strategy that can substitute for disciplined, active management. Even so, senior managers and the business press too often get caught up with new-and-improved solutions and strategies, supposedly proven at some Fortune 500/Global 2000 companies. This is great public relations, but it ignores the realities that managers face on a day-to-day basis, which are critical factors in the success needed to grow corporate value. Far too many of the new-and-improved solutions are based primarily on the experiences of particular companies at particular times. At best, adopting these solutions might enable your company to be a follower; at worst, you might put your company at risk by assuming that what worked elsewhere will necessarily be as or more successful for you. It is rare that you can easily exchange and wear someone else's clothes, yet it seems that companies are willing to assume that what fits at another company will work with minimum customization for them.

Keep in mind that just as insufficient or improper analysis can lead to poor investment decision making, too much analysis can also be detrimental to the investment process. Managers made many poor investments in search of revenue growth in the 1990s, especially IT investments that were insufficiently analyzed and vetted. At the other end of the spectrum, however, overanalyzing investments can lead to what some people call "analysis paralysis," with the result that a company makes minimal investments for the future and will invariably decline. There is also the simple fact, as noted earlier, of politics. Many of us have had the experience of seeing an investment made because a senior manager wanted it done, even if the facts available did not support it.

Who Should Read This Book

This book has important implications for any manager responsible for making investment decisions, executing investments or for proposing investments within his or her company. Using the Business Investment Road-map will help:

- CEOs and CFOs lead organizations to more productive and effective investments that increase returns to stakeholders.

- CIOs, CTOs, and senior members of their staffs establish priorities, support organizational strategies, and prepare business cases for review by senior-level finance staff and executives.

- R&D managers develop objectives and agendas, track and manage R&D investment opportunities, and prepare business cases for finance staff and executives.

- Marketing and HRM managers develop the business case for your initiatives.

- Project managers achieve the holy grail of investments completed on time, on budget, and at the quality and scope levels required by your organization.

- Product and service vendors provide empirically positive returns to your customers, beyond just financial benefits.

What Follows

Chapter 2 provides a formal introduction to the five steps in the Business Investment Roadmap™. The chapters that follow discuss each of the five elements in detail. Chapter 3 provides a detailed discussion of *preliminary analysis,* and is premised on the critical question of whether or not the investment will provide long-term growth and value to your company. Chapter 4 is devoted to the analysis of *business impact analysis,* where you determine the primary drivers of value in your company. Chapter 5 focuses on *risk analysis* and stresses the importance of identifying the major risks your investment faces and the development of a risk mitigation plan. Chapter 6 discusses *execution analysis,* where you determine the who, what, why, where, how, and when needed for an investment, as well as other critical factors that will make the investment successful. Chapter 7 is devoted to *ongoing management,* where you monitor progress and take corrective action when, and if needed, to ensure that your investments will result in growing corporate value. Chapter 8 pulls together the discussion in the earlier chapters.

You will find at the end of several of the chapters a section called "Following the Roadmap" that gives more detailed examples of how to apply the Business Investment Roadmap using a sample company. Depending on your specific interests and needs, as well as the time you have available, the sections at the end of the chapters will provide you working examples of the Business Investment Roadmap to use as a template in your company. The sample company in these sections is called Fresh Breeze, a manufacturer and distributor of personal care and household cleaning products. It is a composite based on financial data from similar companies in the industry. The Appendix reviews some elements of accounting and finance that might be of help to you when you apply the Business Investment Roadmap at your company.

Thank you for taking the time to read this book. We know that what follows will be of value to you and your company, and we appreciate any comments and suggestions you can offer as you put the Business Investment Roadmap to work in your company.

2

GROWING VALUE WITH THE BUSINESS INVESTMENT ROADMAP

"You have chosen wisely."

Holy Grail Knight to Indiana Jones,
Indiana Jones and The Last Crusade

If you set out to build a better mousetrap, you wouldn't start in a vacuum. Instead, you would deconstruct and examine prior models to see which components worked successfully and which needed improvement. Likewise, to improve your company's performance in choosing and executing investments, you must analyze the company's history. Ask yourself these questions:

- Does my company make consistently good investment decisions?

- Whether or not investments turn out well overall, are the original objectives achieved?

- Are we frequently forced to lower our expectations once investments are in progress?

- Do unforeseen events or underlying factors frequently reduce the ultimate value of investments from our original projections?

- Are there triggers or factors that seem to be associated with successful investments that grow shareholder value? Are there triggers or factors that seem to lead to investments that fail? You should be looking for patterns and trends here.

In the popular adventure movie *Indiana Jones and the Last Crusade*, Indiana (played by Harrison Ford) must choose the Holy Grail from among a table full of chalices. If he picks the Holy Grail, both he and his father (played by Sean Connery) will live; if he takes the wrong cup, they both will die. Through a combination of insight, skill, and luck, he chooses the correct cup. Choosing investments also requires insight, skill, and luck, but fortunately the stakes involved in making investment choices are not usually quite as high!

Peter Drucker, perhaps the preeminent business management consultant, once wrote, "There is no better way to improve an organization's performance than to measure the results of capital appropriations against the promises and expectations that led to their authorization." In his book *On Measuring Corporate Performance*, Drucker is clearly right: The investment and spending decisions managers make can have a profound effect on overall corporate performance. This book builds on Drucker's advice by providing a framework for evaluating the financial impact of previous investment decisions and for improving the decision-making process and, therefore, the success rate of future investments.

Companies must constantly make decisions about investments. They are limited by budgets, time, and other resource constraints that force them to choose certain investments from a field of many different possibilities. A badly chosen investment that ends in failure hurts a company in two ways. First, there are the direct losses associated with the resources and time directly spent on the investment. Second, there is the opportunity cost the company suffers by devoting resources to an investment that fails and diverting those resources away from other, potentially more productive investments. Bad investment decisions come with both direct and opportunity costs.

As discussed in Chapter 1, choosing good investments is not enough; they only create value if you execute them properly. Your business mission is twofold: first, you must choose investments that provide you with the best potential returns. Second, you must execute those investments well to achieve the expected returns. Recognizing that no amount of planning can foresee every nuance and turn of events, you must put in place mechanisms to evaluate the performance of the investment, and you must have the flexibility to alter the execution plans to adjust to a constantly changing reality. In other words, for knockout investments, you must deliver the one–two punch of financial analysis and strong execution skills to bridge the execution gap.

Using the Business Investment Roadmap

The Business Investment Roadmap will help you bridge the execution gap. The Roadmap gives you a formal, step-by-step framework for evaluating and executing new investment opportunities. You can apply the Roadmap consistently to investment management across your company, and you will create shareholder value and improve the financial performance of your company. Although the Business Investment Roadmap is not a one-size-fits-all approach, it is extremely flexible. Today's world is rapidly changing; the assumptions you start with when you decide to proceed with an investment can, and usually do, change during the course of its execution. The Business Investment Roadmap allows you the flexibility to anticipate changes and respond appropriately to them.

You might already use some of the analytical tools that make up the Business Investment Roadmap, whereas others will be less familiar. Together, these tools are integrated into a formalized, disciplined, and consistent approach geared specifically to analyzing investments.

The Business Investment Roadmap has five sequential elements, summarized in Figure 2.1, each with its own set of analytical tools. Each element asks you to dig progressively deeper into the investments you are considering. As you proceed through the elements, therefore, you are applying increasingly stringent filters to the investment. This approach has two benefits. First, you can eliminate the obviously bad investments at once. Thus, you can focus your efforts better as you analyze the remaining investment options with increasing scrutiny. Second, the Business Investment Roadmap might highlight ways to change or improve an investment to increase its potential returns and the likelihood that you will achieve those returns. Your company will be investing in a series of steps or options, rather than an all-or-nothing investment. This is analogous to the difference between climbing down the stairs and jumping off a cliff. Finally, the Roadmap follows investments from beginning to end, because some investments will make it through the vetting process but will require alteration or termination after they are underway. The sequential nature of the Business Investment Roadmap analysis helps you to screen out unwise investments as early as possible and to avoid wasted time, effort, and resources.

The five elements of the Business Investment Roadmap are like successive layers of an onion. Each layer gets you deeper into the onion, as each step gets you deeper into the investment. The investment may no longer look promising when under closer scru-

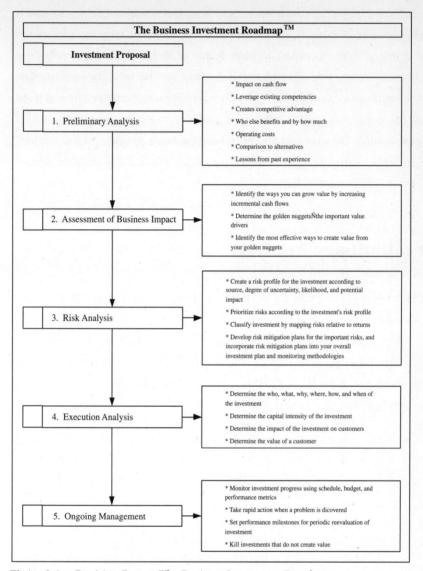

Figure 2.1 Decision Route: The Business Investment Roadmap

tiny; in the onion analogy, your eyes might water too much to continue. At that point, it does not make sense to peel off additional layers; it is time to move on to other ingredients (investments) to achieve your goals.

Each element includes a series of analytical questions and issues to consider. Focus on the elements most relevant to your objectives and goals. For example, if your team is responsible for evaluating business cases, you should focus mainly on the first three elements. If your team is asked to implement an investment after the decision to go ahead, then you should focus on the last two elements. If your team is involved in the entire investment process, from evaluation and promotion to execution, you should follow the entire Business Investment Roadmap.

Preliminary Analysis

The preliminary analysis is the first layer of the onion. It is meant to quickly screen out obviously bad or inappropriate investments. It takes you through some basic questions and issues to determine whether the investment is likely to have a positive effect on incremental cash flows. The preliminary analysis helps you to examine these questions:

- How does the investment impact cash flow? It is critical to predict quantitatively the costs of an investment and the benefits the investment is expected to provide for the company in terms of incremental cash flows.

- How does the investment leverage existing competencies at your company? All other things being equal, an investment that builds on the competencies already present at your company has a better chance of success and of better returns, than an investment that requires your company to develop entirely new competencies.

- How does the investment increase your company's competitive advantage? To create long-term or sustainable value, an investment must increase the competitive advantages your company enjoys; otherwise, the benefits of the investment will be rather short-lived.

- How do other organizations benefit from your investment and by how much? Investments can have unintended effects that must be examined; if an investment benefits your competitors more than it benefits your own company, you should not pursue it!

- What are the operating costs associated with the investment once it is completed? These long-term operating costs must be considered when you project the benefits and net incremental cash flows of an investment.

- How does this investment compare to other investment alternatives? Because your company has limited resources, it is forced to choose constantly between competing investments. Any investment decision must take into consideration the other investment opportunities that your company is choosing *not* to pursue by devoting resources to this particular investment.

- What are the lessons learned from past experiences at your company and in your industry? These lessons can both point out the pitfalls of the investment and provide a reality check on the assumptions underlying the cash flow projections for this investment.

The investment's proponents or champions should know the answers to these questions. With their help, you can proceed relatively quickly through the preliminary analysis and decide whether to explore the investment in more detail or rule it out as unproductive.

The preliminary analysis also helps you to consider the investment in the context of the company's overall portfolio of investments. With the exception of startup ventures, most companies have numerous ongoing investments simultaneously. Some of these investments will inevitably fail to perform up to expectations; some will exceed expectations. Because of the critical nature of overall balance among your investments, as part of the preliminary analysis you need to assess each investment opportunity to ensure that you have appropriate balance. You don't want to put all of your eggs in one basket, so you should avoid investments with identical or simultaneous success and risk factors. Consider Lucent Technologies, a former high-flyer in the stock market. During the telecom boom in the late 1990s, Lucent acquired Kenan Systems, a telecommunications industry billing software supplier, for approximately $1.3 billion. Two years later, Lucent sold Kenan to CSG Systems for less than $275 million, a loss of more than $1 billion to the company. The factors driving the success and business at Kenan were primarily the same as those for other Lucent businesses, and when the "perfect storm" came, Lucent stakeholders took a major hit. Although Lucent recently announced its first profitable quarter in more than three years, its stock still trades at less than 10 percent of its value during the boom.

There are innumerable examples of companies that could have avoided major investment failures simply by going through this simple preliminary analysis. Take Priceline.com, for instance. The company's major core business was, and continues to be, "name your own price" airline tickets and, to a lesser extent, hotel reservations. Priceline's ads, featuring William Shatner, the "name your own price" concept, and the myriad of problems the company has endured with this business model are legendary, but the travel business does provide the company with the bulk of its operating revenues. At the height of the Internet bubble, Priceline founder Jay Walker created an affiliate company called Webclub House to sell consumer products such as groceries and gasoline with a similar "name your own price" approach. Through this company, customers placed bids on product categories, and Webclub House would get back to them to tell them whether their price had been accepted and for which brand at which store chain. The customer would then pick up the items at the retailer that had accepted the bid. The company planned to rely on manufacturers to absorb the cost of the discounts required to attract and keep customers on the site. Manufacturers, it argued, would get brand loyalty and customer shopping data in return.

Unfortunately, many of the larger manufacturers did not sign up for the business, and Webclub was forced to subsidize the cost of the groceries. Although a large number of people used the service, nearly every sale was made at a loss, and there was no short-term or even medium-term way out of the loss column in sight. Priceline eventually pulled the plug on this affiliate business, but not before the company burned through $360 million in venture capital in less than a year.

There were too many problems with the Webclub House approach and its subsequent execution to name a single showstopper. Customers were extremely expensive to acquire, and yet, there was a high churn rate. The technology architecture the company used in its rush to get the service out was not easy to scale in response to customer demand. The value proposition for customers was difficult to understand. The process of using the Webclub House service was complicated and cumbersome. It offered little to customers but the prospect of a better price. The value proposition for retailers and manufacturers alike was not attractive enough to get them signed up, particularly for manufacturers, who were supposed to provide the bulk of the discount on the groceries. The data model used by the company made it difficult to segregate prices by geographic region. After a year in business, the company was no closer to achieving operational break-even; thus, additional cash infusions were constantly necessary to compensate for the bleeding from operations. Finally, all of this complexity was piled on top of a business (grocery distribution and retail) that has notoriously thin margins.

Webclub House as a business had many holes. A preliminary analysis like the one suggested in this book would have uncovered many of these problems on the drawing board. It could have saved investors many millions of dollars lost in a business that had no legitimate chance of success.

Priceline escaped from its grocery fiasco with *only* $360 million in losses. Although dwarfed by the miserable telecommunications investments of the 1990s, the investments that were poured into variations of grocery delivery services are astounding. WebVan alone burned through about $1 billion, and at the time there were several other companies making similar large-scale investments: Kozmo, HomeGrocer, and Streamline to name a few. Applying the preliminary analysis would have saved investors the hundreds of millions of dollars lost.

Assessment of Business Impact

If your investment makes the preliminary analysis cut, that means it will provide a positive impact on cash flows, it passes muster relative to past investments at the company and within your industry, and it does not have the same risk and return profile as other ongoing investments. The next step requires you to peel back another layer of the onion, to determine *specifically* the major value drivers of your company and the degree to which the investment will provide those positive cash flows through those value drivers. The Business Investment Roadmap calls these major value drivers *golden nuggets*. These golden nuggets are the areas where your company is going to create most of its future value and generate most of its future profits; thus, it is important that the investments you choose focus on these areas, rather than areas that are not critical value drivers. Determining your company's value drivers at such a level of granularity allows you to determine what Jim Collins describes as the "key insight" for reaching your company's "economic denominator," in his book *Good to Great*. This granularity is also critical to establishing what Robert Kaplan and David Norton refer to as "strategic financial themes," in *The Balanced Scorecard*.

Assessing the business impact for a specific investment is extremely important because the value of an investment varies by industry, by company within an industry, and with the overall business environment. What works for one or more of your competitors might not be of much value to you, depending on the macro economy, your position in the market, and the key factors driving your business.

Here is a quick example to consider: Gillette is in the business of selling razor blades, not razors; in other words, the golden nugget for the company is from sales of replacement razor blades. A customer buys the razor only once, but Gillette gets the vast majority of its profits as recurring revenues, as the customer replaces razor blades when they wear out. A few years ago, the prior management team at Gillette diversified the company into other businesses that, in retrospect, were not as profitable as razor blades. The new management team has since made major changes, including divesting the company of a number of noncore businesses. Current management is more likely to devote time and effort to investments that make the production and sales of razor blades more efficient and profitable rather than other opportunities.

Printer cartridges play a similar role at Hewlett Packard (HP). Although HP is a technology leader and one of the top PC manufacturers, its primary source of profits is the printer business. Within the printer division, the ink cartridges provide most of HP's profits.

As most of us well know, ink cartridges empty quickly (particularly when you don't have time to get another one) and customers replacing cartridges provides a source of recurring revenue and profits for HP. The ink cartridge business figured prominently in HP's merger with Compaq. There was an acrimonious fight between senior HP managers, who openly supported the merger with Compaq, and the children of HP's founders, who opposed the deal. One of the issues raised by opponents of the merger was that the acquisition of Compaq would take resources and management attention away from the company's primary golden nuggets, printers and printer cartridges. Whether this merger ultimately creates or erodes value at HP remains to be seen, but the company definitely has taken a risk by diverting resources away from its golden nuggets.

Risk Analysis

After you have determined the critical value drivers of your company and ensured that the investment you are considering is in line with those value drivers, you need to peel down even further by focusing attention on the critical trade-off between risk and return. From your personal investments, you are probably familiar with the idea that with greater returns come greater risks. If you are risk-averse in your selection of investments, the returns on your investments will be more predictable, but they will have less potential upside. Savings accounts are safe and insured by the Federal Deposit Insurance Corporation (FDIC), an arm of the federal government, but the returns are very low. Investments in equities offer the potential of much higher returns, but you face the risk that you will lose your entire investment. You can reduce some of this risk by diversifying your equity investments through mutual funds or other means. By creating a portfolio of investments, you are more likely to counterbalance a complete loss in one investment with gains in others.

Corporate investments are like personal ones; very few provide high returns with low risk. Such low-risk, high-return investments are usually too good to be true. From statistics, you might remember means (the average) and standard deviations (the range from the average, like the sides of a bell curve). Another way to think about the trade-off between risk and return is that you trade a higher mean (return) for a much smaller standard deviation (the range of what you can lose or gain), as shown in Figure 2.2, which compares a high-risk, high-return investment and a low-risk, low-return investment.

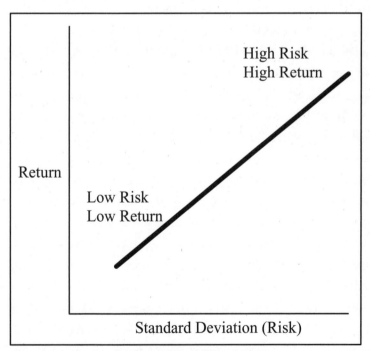

Figure 2.2   The Trade-Off Between Risk and Return

This risk and return assessment also applies in business; it is the third step in the Business Investment Roadmap. You cannot afford to wait around for the rare investment with low risks and high returns. What you do need is a set of analytical tools that you can apply consistently to different kinds of investments. At the level of your overall corporate growth and value creation strategy, you can treat investments like a portfolio, such that the failure of one investment will hopefully be outweighed by gains in others. Obviously, in the context of a single investment, such as a software system, you cannot mitigate the risk by investing redundantly in several systems; resources are too limited. Nevertheless, you can try to make sure that your company has several options overall for growth and value creation.

The Business Investment Roadmap gives you a consistent risk analysis methodology that you can apply to every investment opportunity you consider. This methodology rates risks on several different criteria: source, level of uncertainty, likelihood of occurrence, and the impact on the investment if a particular risk does occur. Using these criteria, you can determine the most important risks involved in the investment and develop mitigation or contingency plans to deal with those risks. Collecting this information for each important risk facing an investment also allows you to develop a risk profile for that investment. By comparing this risk profile to the expected returns of the investment, you can decide whether the returns of the investment are sufficient to assume its risks.

Iridium provides a textbook example of ignoring business risks. The company started with an interesting, but as it turned out, uneconomical, implausible, and completely unnecessary idea that ended in one of the biggest business fiascoes ever. Iridium had its origins in the 1980s; it was originally proposed by engineers at Motorola as a global satellite wireless phone network. The system, which was to have a total of 66 satellites, promised to connect subscribers anywhere in the world. Ten years and $7 billion after it was formally announced, Iridium fell apart. Among its many problems, Iridium ignored a great many risks in pursuing this global telecommunications network so ambitiously. The idea was based on a technology that became largely obsolete over the course of a 10-year period due to advances in cellular telecommunications technology. These advances obviated many of Iridium's benefits.

The Iridium technology also did not work exactly as promised; the phone had to be used in the open air because it did not work well inside buildings. The company did not properly gauge or approach the risk that its potential customers would not adopt the technology. The cost of its service exceeded alternative technologies by a significant margin. Finally, to succeed, the company needed 500,000 subscribers. At the time it shut down, it had only 55,000 customers. A proper risk analysis and risk mitigation plan might not have saved Iridium, but it could have stemmed some of the losses if the company had focused on a more stepwise approach to the investment.

Execution Analysis

The fourth element of the Business Investment Roadmap is execution analysis. You need to determine the who, what, when, where, why, and how of an investment so that it will produce the promised returns in revenue, growth, and corporate value. This process is critical to success because it is where you bridge the gap between strategy and financial metrics. Execution issues are, by definition, the "devil in the details" that we often hear about. This is where you have peeled very deeply into the onion. You might inevitably cause lots of tears among the proponents of the investment by forcing them to provide the details of the investment, rather than letting them simply pass them off until later on, after the investment has been approved. Explanations such as "we will figure that out later" or "that's simple, you need to focus on the big picture" are not acceptable.

Imagine you are about to travel by car from Los Angeles to Boston. Prior to setting out, you would likely go through a checklist of items, including confirming that the car is ready for the trip, making hotel reservations, acquiring maps, obtaining sufficient cash, and attending to other details to ensure a safe and relatively risk-free journey. If you are especially detail-oriented, you might go even further, stocking up on food and entertainment for passengers (especially if you are bringing children). These actions would help ensure the success of your journey as well as minimize downtime at rest stops and restaurants.

Evaluating an investment at your company requires you to prepare the same type of detailed analysis and review as you would for your car trip from Los Angeles to Boston. You need to think about and work closely with the proponents of the investment to determine and to define operationally your milestones and required resources. Unlike the car trip, however, you must go much deeper into your review to develop detailed operational and work plans. These plans can both confirm the viability of the investment and provide a baseline against which you can track performance as the investment proceeds. You must consider complexity issues, capital intensity, and the lessons learned from past experience at a more detailed level than before. There are always new mistakes to be made, but "lessons learned" files can at least help you avoid repeating mistakes.

Keep in mind that determining the who, what, when, where, why, and how of an investment does not lock you into a single, inflexible path. Plans are meant to change in response to circumstances. In the road trip analogy, there is no reason you could not change the route you take from Los Angeles to Boston in response to a new opportunity, to visit a special place, or to avoid major road construction.

Determining the who, what, when, where, why, and how of an investment in the beginning is just that, a start that will probably require changes as the investment plays out. Head coaches in the National Football League typically script the first 15 or 20 plays for their team prior to the game, which helps the team to prepare, execute well, and get into the groove of the game. Coaches have a set plan for the beginning of the game, but as it unfolds, they adjust to what is happening on the field. This approach gives them the flexibility to make changes that fit the changing circumstances of the game. Ideally, an investment plan will follow a similar pattern. The investment is analyzed and the game plan is set up at the beginning, but the execution plan needs to be flexible enough to adjust to changing conditions and to the new realities that emerge as the investment plays out.

Finally, execution analysis requires you to examine the effect of an investment on your customer base. Any benefits projected to result from an investment are premised on your ability to retain your customers; thus, it is critical to look at both the direct and indirect effects a given investment might have on customers. Similarly, it is important to understand the value of your customers, to determine both the impact of losing certain customers and what your company should be willing to pay to acquire new customers.

Ongoing Management

Once your investment has successfully passed the first four analysis hurdles and you have decided to proceed with it, ongoing management is the next and final step. Ongoing management helps to ensure that your investment provides the promised returns. You must develop and apply metrics to evaluate investment performance quickly. Developing the proper metrics to measure investment performance is often difficult. Everyone knows that it is important to have metrics for time and budgets, but it is just as important to have metrics that track what is being delivered (or performed) and those that measure factors unique to the investment. Imagine you are planning a home renovation project. Once you and the contractor agree to work together, the contractor will expect payments for work that is completed. Although the contractor might disagree, you would not want to base those payments on a percentage of the total project costs and time alone but on the work that is actually done. For example, you would not pay the contractor 50 percent of the total project cost for a six-month project at the three-month point, unless she or he has accomplished what you both had agreed to be the marker or milestones at three months.

Corporate investments need to be treated the same way as the home renovation project. Unfortunately, managers often measure progress primarily by time and budgets and do not consider sufficiently what has been accomplished. By evaluating the investment on the basis of schedule, cost, and *performance,* you ensure that your company gets what it expected.

Ongoing management also involves periodic reviews of the investment from the perspective of the assumptions and reasons underlying your original assessment. As the investment progresses, you will gain more knowledge and have a better sense of its ultimate likelihood of success. Business conditions change, and the assumptions in your original evaluation should change in response. This is when changes can and should be made to the expected deliverables (i.e., performance), time, and budget. If appropriate, you must be prepared to take corrective actions, including ending the investment entirely.

Imagine that your company has embarked on an R&D effort for a new product. The investment takes two years, and, at about month 20, when the viability of the product has been proven in market tests and you are preparing for a major launch, a competitor enters the marketplace with a product that has attributes that are superior to those of your product. This new information would clearly alter your original assumptions and analysis; it might cause you to decide to stop work and write off the investment made over the past 20 months, even if the team at your company has met their milestones on time, on budget, and in terms of expected performance.

Will the Business Investment Roadmap Guarantee Success?

You will find the Business Investment Roadmap to be a valuable resource when you evaluate and execute business investments. You will not need to go through every step in equal detail for every investment, but the Business Investment Roadmap will allow you and your company to make smarter and more profitable decisions. Your investment decisions will be wisely chosen and based on a disciplined and consistent methodology built on a mastery of business basics. Keep in mind that although the Business Investment Roadmap can help you to grow corporate value, use of it does not guarantee success. Unlike Indiana Jones, you and your company might not always choose wisely, even using the Roadmap.

The Business Investment Roadmap is a complement to, but not a substitute for, traditional, finance-driven, analytical techniques. You still need to be comfortable with some accounting and finance, as well as general business principles, to make sound investments that will grow corporate value. You do not need to be an accountant or someone with formal training in finance to use the Roadmap. You will still be able use the strategies described in this book. To help you put the Business Investment Roadmap to work immediately, you will find "Following the Roadmap" sections in Chapters 3 through 7 and in the Appendix. These sections review some basic accounting and finance concepts, explain the fundamental analysis involved in the Business Investment Roadmap in more detail, and apply the Roadmap to a composite consumer products company, Fresh Breeze, a manufacturer of detergents, personal cleaning products, and air fresheners. The company is based in Chicago and has manufacturing plants throughout the United States.

3

PRELIMINARY ANALYSIS

*The White Rabbit put on his spectacles. "Where
shall I begin, please your Majesty?" he asked.*

*"Begin at the beginning," the King said gravely,
and "go on till you come to the end: then stop."*

Lewis Carroll, Alice in Wonderland

The first element in the Business Investment Roadmap is the
preliminary analysis, as shown in Figure 3.1. The preliminary
examination offers six questions to frame your analysis of an
investment. A good first step is to ask the proponents of an investment
to answer these six questions. Keep in mind that proponents, by
nature, tend to be enthusiastic about an investment; they might not be
objective enough to see anything that does not support the investment,
even if such weaknesses are obvious to an outside reviewer. Also be
sure to check the information that they use to answer the questions.
As always, be mindful of situations where the proponents are in a
position politically where they can drive the decision to make the
investment, no matter what the merits of the investment are.

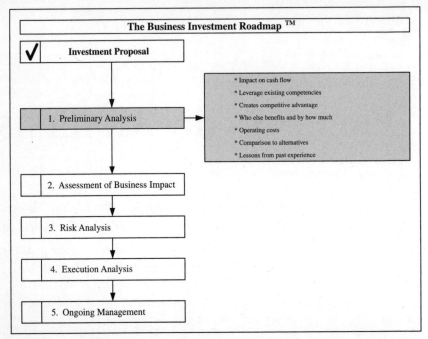

Figure 3.1   Decision Route: The Business Investment Roadmap Preliminary Analysis

Let's proceed through the six questions for the analysis as listed in Figure 3.2.

1. Assume That We Make This investment and It Is Successful. What Will Be the Impact on the Company's Cash Flow?

This question seems so simple and obvious that you might wonder why it is here, let alone as the first question. It is first because it is the most important question; it is the fundamental basis of analyzing investments. For example, imagine that you are considering an investment in equipment that will enable you to reduce your costs of providing customer support by 10 percent through improvements in support staff efficiency and productivity. The vendor shows you that this equipment has yielded an ROI in excess of 200 percent at other

Six Questions to Ask an Investment's Proponents

Assume that we make this investment and it is successful.

1. What will be the impact on the company's cash flow?

2. Will this investment leverage our existing competencies and help to create a competitive advantage?

3. Who else benefits and how much of the benefits from the investment do they receive?

4. What is the long-term committment? How much cash will we need to devote to the investment on an operating basis after the initial investment is completed?

Assume we want to make this investment but cannot.

5. What is the next best alternative?

6. Is there anything we can do differently that gets us nearly the same benefits in cash flow returns to the company?

Figure 3.2   Six Questions to Ask Investment Proponents

companies. This investment appears to be a certain winner, so why not proceed with it right away to ensure that your company can start enjoying the benefits as soon as possible?

Here's why. A quick review of your company's income statement indicates that customer support costs represent about 5 percent of total expenses. Even if this investment works and provides the high ROI exactly as promised, it will, at best, reduce total expenses by about 0.5 percent (customer support costs of 5 percent are reduced by 10 percent; 10 percent of 5 percent is 0.5 percent). The 0.5 percent reduction assumes the *very best* scenario; the investment is implemented without any hitches and it performs precisely as represented by the vendor; even though we all know that the execution of investments seldom goes exactly as planned. Also, you have not even considered whether the returns to the company are easily and objectively measured or more subjective (e.g., increased morale). In addition, the vendor's claim assumes that the benefits in savings will be in cash outlays, which will have to come from a reduction in the salaries paid to customer service representatives through layoffs, lower wages, or reduced hours for each representative. The vendor's analysis conveniently excludes critical questions related to what happens to the service representatives who cannot find another position in the company. For example what about the costs of the layoffs and decreased morale?

Even putting aside these issues that the vendor doesn't talk about, the bottom line impact to the company is relatively minimal. With this kind of relatively low bang for the buck, why bother? Keep the checkbook closed; your company's valuable resources would be better spent elsewhere. Your analysis is complete; it is time to move on to activities that will provide a better return to your company in higher profits and growing corporate value.

This simple focus on the impact on company cash flows for every type of investment opportunity might be a major reason decision makers at many companies are simply saying no to investments. Their view might be that even if the investments are successful and the vendors' products do provide a high return on the dollars invested, the impact on incremental cash flows just is not enough to make the effort.

Alternatively, assume that the impact on incremental cash flows will be significant. Going back to the example of an investment in equipment that reduces customer support expenses, let's assume that customer support costs represent 30 percent of your expenses and the savings from the investment will reduce spending for salaries and, thus, increase bottom line cash flows. The investment now would result in cutting your total expenses by about 1.5 percent. In today's increasingly competitive marketplace, this investment might be worth making, particularly in industries in which profit margins are low. In contrast, if profit margins are relatively high in your industry and company, then 1.5 percent might not be sufficient to justify pursuing the investment.

The Incremental Cash Flows Are What Matter: The preceding example focuses on the importance of evaluating investments in terms of incremental cash flows. It is the cash flows that will sustain growth in corporate value, and all investments need to be tracked in terms of the impact on incremental cash flows. This focus applies even for the relatively rare investments that have potentially high returns with low risk "on paper," when the investments are being proposed. When considering these types of investments, you need to determine whether the projected revenue gains are realistic and whether those gains will actually produce incremental cash flows. You also need to determine if the investment returns really are low risk. Consider, for example, Johnson & Johnson, a global company that provides products ranging from Band-Aids and Tylenol to very sophisticated medical instruments used in noninvasive surgery. The investment would be for the development of a new type of bandage that can be used in the home, one that helps to seal minor cuts while providing protection against infection. In this case, they would need to drill down on the assumptions regarding the revenue opportunity (size of the market and its growth rate) and confirm by looking at the income statements of other companies offering similar products that the projected cash flows are realistic. In this example, Johnson & Johnson would have the benefit of using data on sales from its regular Band-Aid products as a reference point when projecting incremental cash flows.

2. Will This Investment Leverage Our Existing Competencies and Help to Create a Competitive Advantage?

Many of us are familiar with the saying that you need to walk before you can run, and crawl before you can walk. The same logic applies when we evaluate investment opportunities. Companies often make investments before their people and processes are capable of assimilating them, and, as a result, they are unable to attain the promised benefits. As an example, think about the massive investments many companies have made in enterprise resource planning (ERP) software without appropriate investments to change their processes and prepare their staffs for organizational changes. Many ERP projects failed, primarily because of the lack of sufficient investments in infrastructure, process change, and lack of staff support for organizational change. (Many companies offering enterprise-level software, including sales force automation software, now provide their products via the Web, significantly reducing the up-front investment in time and resources needed when companies had to load and configure software on their own systems, or else simply would not make the investment in hardware. Seibel, for example, has now begun offering its software as an applications services provider [ASP].)

Most of us are creatures of habit, and it is difficult to get us to change. Changing the procedures and processes in a business is even more complex and difficult, especially because the company has to continue with normal business activities during the transition. Some people describe this challenge as akin to changing the transmission in a car while it is going 60 miles per hour. It is not an easy task, and often is more likely to fail than succeed.

As a manager, you cannot count on the fact that an investment will achieve the returns you expect unless your organization is fully prepared to accept and grow from those changes. You need to have the infrastructure in place—at a minimum the people and physical assets—to gain the benefits from an investment. For example, many HRM-driven efforts to improve morale and performance of sales staff fail because compensation systems are not realigned to reinforce the messages and reward people for the adoption of the new ways of doing business.

This process is, of course, much easier said than done. Often changes in compensation plans spur many people who were comfortable under the old structure to leave. Recently, for example, one of the nation's leading retailers of electronics products, Circuit City, decided to change the ways that it sold products in response to continued declines in the price and profit margins of electronics products. Rather than having commissioned salespeople work closely with prospective customers, the company decided to move to more of a self-service system. In response to this change, the company altered the compensation structure for its sales representatives from commissions to straight salary. Many of the more successful salespeople under the old system have since left the company.

Similarly, many management and IT consultants seek to have their clients recognize the importance of making investments that fit within the overall corporate strategy or what is often called "business model" or "business design." Adrian Slywotzky and David Morrison with Karl Weber, in their book *How Digital Is Your Business?* focus on this issue.[1] They show that it is not technology that drives higher growth and returns, but business models and the use of technology to support those business models. Other researchers have found no positive relationship between investments in technology and increased returns to shareholders (unless you count the shareholders of the companies making the sales).

---

1. Adrian J. Slywotzky, David J. Morrison, with Karl Webber, *How Digital Is Your Business?* (New York: Crown Business, 2000).

Think again about the Los Angeles-to-Boston road trip introduced in the last chapter. You are driving on the highway and making great time to your destination. Now, you leave the highway in favor of more scenic, local roads, and quickly fall behind schedule; the local roads simply are not sufficient to handle the traffic. The bottleneck is not the highway, but the local roads. Business works in much the same way. Your company should not make investments if it does not have the infrastructure or corporate capabilities and business model that can benefit fully from those investments.

Wal-Mart provides a great example of matching investments with corporate capabilities. Wal-Mart is the global leader in the use of technology (in fact, a recent study found that a significant portion of the total gains in productivity in the U.S. economy during the 1990s was due to Wal-Mart), but the company will only invest when it can easily integrate the new technologies into its existing infrastructure. Disruptions are minimal, and the new technology acts like a turbocharger, rather than as a replacement for existing business processes.

Obviously, it is difficult to answer directly the question of whether your company has the infrastructure and competencies to support an investment. On one hand, it is easy to say "yes," and assume that your company can leverage the investment into a competitive advantage. That is the answer you will get from the proponents of the investment who will sing its praises to you. Accordingly, you must ask them to define as clearly and succinctly as possible the *unique* capabilities of your organization compared to your competitors and exactly how this investment will create a competitive advantage within your business model.

Consider Apple Computer's recent investment in an online distribution system for music. Steve Jobs, one of the founders of Apple and once again the CEO, leveraged his relationships in the music industry to enable Apple to establish distribution relationships with several major music labels. In the meantime, the company created an online distribution system for music that provides a way to source and download music at a cost of 99 cents per song. Apple's system is, of course, legitimate and legal as compared with the free services that have been subject to lawsuits and other actions by the music industry seeking to close them down.

Although it is still early in the life cycle of the business, Apple's investment has, by most accounts, been a success. More than a million songs were downloaded during the first week that the Apple system was available to the public. Apple's investment clearly leveraged its competencies, and it has given the company at least a temporary competitive advantage that will add revenue and profits to the bottom line. More important, however, the online music business will likely drive sales of the Apple iPod, which is where the company will gain substantially more revenues and profits in comparison to its online music sales.

On the other hand, Microsoft and the major hardware providers like IBM, Dell, and HP are not likely to go into the online music distribution business on their own. The business of selling music over the Internet is simply too small of an opportunity at this time in terms of potential revenue dollars without having the revenue streams and profits from hardware like the Apple iPod. They might, however, get into the business of selling hardware like Apple's iPod.

If your competitors can easily match the investment you are considering, the investment might not provide competitive advantage. Instead, it might simply be part of the ante required to compete. This fact is particularly relevant in industries with commodity or near-commodity products and services. This leads you to the next question.

3. Assume That We Make This Investment and It Is Successful. Who Else Benefits, and How Much of the Benefits from the Investment Do They Get?

This question prompts you to think about whether the benefits from the investment will really result in an increase in revenues, profits, cash flow, and corporate value. Recall the prior example of the company that invested in a customer support system, and the importance of confirming that savings would result in higher incremental cash flows. If the investment in customer support makes your customer support staff more efficient, what does this mean in terms of tangible expense reductions to the company? Will the customer support staff work at the higher productivity level for the same pay? Can the company assume a reduction in the number of staff personnel through attrition? If so, when will the people leave, and how do you consider those cost reductions in your analysis? Is the market so competitive that your investment in providing more efficient customer support results in your staff devoting more time and resources on average to customer inquiries? This could render the investment worthwhile for corporate goodwill but not create a positive bottom line impact. In other words, would the company attract users that require more service and are, thus, likely to be less profitable customers?

Consider the investment that your neighborhood bank made for automated teller machines (ATMs). A transaction handled by an ATM is significantly less expensive than a transaction handled by a teller, and ATMs are available 24/7. These are direct benefits to customers. Nevertheless, ATMs cannot and will not replace tellers; instead, ATMs are simply *expected* by customers in addition to fast and efficient service by tellers. Several years ago many people associated with the banking industry assumed that ATMs and electronic banking would make branches, those high-cost vestiges of past banking practices, obsolete. Some banks went so far as to close branches and replace them with a wall of ATMs. More recently, banks recognized that ATMs were not a substitute for branches, but simply another way of doing business. The recent decision by Bank of America to acquire Fleet Bank, the leading commercial and consumer bank in New England, was motivated by Bank of America's desire to gain access to Fleet's branch network. Like branches and electronic banking, ATMs are simply another cost of doing business for commercial banks. Customers have clearly gained from financial institution investments in ATMs, but for the banks, it is an additional investment and ongoing expense.

We see a similar situation with retailers' e-commerce sites. At one time, retailers needed to worry only about the challenges of building and maintaining physical stores. The Internet raised the ante by creating pressure on retailers to establish e-commerce sites. Many retailers invested relatively enormous sums of money and devoted significant amounts of management time to the creation of e-commerce divisions. The threat of being "Amazoned" by retailers that did not have to make investments in physical assets like retail stores added to management pressures. Numerous press reports lavishing praise on Internet pioneers and leaders like Jeff Bezos, the founder of Amazon and *Time Magazine* Man of the Year, likely added fuel to the fire of fear at many retailers.

Today, it is accepted wisdom in retailing that you need both "bricks" (physical stores) and "clicks" (a Web presence), even if your Web site is solely for promotions and background information such as store locations and phone numbers. The e-commerce divisions of some retailers have become profitable, but the vast majority of retailers now see their e-commerce efforts as a cost center that is complementary to and supportive of their physical stores or catalog operations, rather than as a profit center. E-commerce has clearly been a factor to increase customer service and satisfaction. Like ATMs for banks, however, the impact on the bottom line has not been positive for many retailers.

The hotel industry has had similar experiences. Today, a hotel seeking a three-star ranking from either the *Mobile Travel Guide* or the Automobile Association of America (AAA) must provide services and amenities that were considered necessary only for five-star hotels a few years ago. For example, a fluffy bathrobe and comfortable slippers was once standard only at leading hotel chains like Four Seasons or Ritz-Carlton. Today, it is a requirement for earning just a three-star ranking. All of these investments by the lodging chains have made our travel experience better and more comfortable, but the returns to the shareholders of the lodging chain stocks have been minimal.

These are only illustrative examples; the key issue is that you need to determine who else benefits from your investments. As with the investments made by banks in ATMs, investments have to be made for competitive reasons, even with minimal incremental positive impact on the bottom line. It might be, however, that the investments you are evaluating do not provide a direct economic benefit to the company and are not necessarily a requirement to compete.

4. Assume That We Make This Investment and It Is Successful. What Is the Long-Term Commitment? Will We Need to Devote Cash to the Investment on an Operating Basis After the Initial Investment Is Made?

Most investments represent just the down payment on what turns out to be a long-term corporate initiative. Consider General Motors' (GM) investment in Saturn. General Motors decided to create an entirely new car brand in the 1980s. The advertising pitch, both for internal and external purposes, was "a different kind of car company." GM invested more than $1 billion in Saturn and successfully created a new brand, a major accomplishment for any company, but particularly so for GM.

Unfortunately for GM shareholders, Saturn's success has required more investment from GM, not less. GM still has to subsidize Saturn on an operating basis. In an attempt to try and make Saturn more self-sufficient, GM has extended the line of Saturn cars in hopes of growing total volume. Where once Saturn's offerings were primarily sedans, the company now has a full line of cars, including a sport utility vehicle (SUV).

GM's investment in Saturn and the need for ongoing investment is similar to what Ford faces with Jaguar. After investing approximately $500 million to acquire Jaguar, Ford has subsequently had to invest at least that amount to get the company competitive in terms of technology, styling, and reliability of its cars. Although Jaguars are attractive and fun to drive for many people, Ford is now stuck with a major drain on its capital for the foreseeable future, and the marketplace for vehicles in that class is becoming increasingly competitive. Ford also faces a major dilemma in making sure that the use of Ford components in Jaguar is limited, thus limiting opportunities to gain economies of scale in parts. Who wants to open the hood of their brand new Jaguar and see the same parts that are in a Ford Taurus?

There are many other examples where managers have not sufficiently differentiated between initial cash needs to fund an investment and ongoing cash needs. Consider the now outrageous financial projections for the dot-com companies during the late 1990s. Several analysts argued that one of the ways that the high values of some of the dot-com companies on NASDAQ could be justified was that these companies would not require as much capital (cash) for operations once they had built their infrastructure and acquired customers (their initial capital investment needs). In contrast to traditional companies, Internet-based companies were expected to acquire positive cash flow very quickly. This was due to the reduced need for capital on an ongoing basis for operations and would thus provide greater returns to their shareholders than comparable traditional "old economy" companies.

The reality, of course, was just the opposite. Among the surviving dot-coms, most have found that there is a need for additional capital in both fixed assets, such as plant, equipment, and warehouses, and to support inventory and accounts receivable, or what finance and accounting people call *working capital*. Amazon, for example, soon found out that it needed significantly more capital than expected when the company began to open warehouses around the country to reduce shipping times and also expanded beyond books to other products. More recently, Netflix, the first company to rent DVDs via the Internet, had to invest in inventory and warehouses throughout the country to reduce shipping times and improve customer service. Without this investment, the company could not effectively compete with neighborhood Blockbuster video stores.

This question is not just applicable to major industrial companies or the dot-coms. Many of us have had the experience of owning a car, home, or other asset that seems to own us because of the need for additional spending and resource allocation. For most businesses, an initial investment will inevitably result in the need to devote additional resources. Investments are rarely one-time events.

5. Assume We Want to Make This Investment, but Cannot. What Is the Next Best Alternative? Is There Anything We Can Do Differently That Gets Us Nearly the Same Benefits in Cash Flow Returns to the Company?

This question forces the champions of investments to rethink and justify their proposals. It helps you to cut to the chase because it requires a thorough analysis of an investment in the context of other investments that might provide similar benefits. It changes the discussion from a yes or no for a particular investment to a review of alternatives. It will often result in your making a better choice.

The question is applicable for all types of investments. Consider R&D. One of the common refrains in research and development is that "the enemy of good enough is perfect." By investing in the "good enough," you can mitigate some of the risks, such as time to market and development (you will see more about risks in a later chapter), trading off a relatively small part of the financial returns. At General Electric, for example, the new CEO, Jeffrey Immelt, has sought to have the company's research facilities focus on getting products to market faster in lieu of doing too much theoretical research.

Consider this question in the context of mergers and acquisitions. All too often, companies jump into acquisitions when other types of relationships can provide the same benefits without the hassles and costs of putting two companies together. In the AOL Time-Warner deal, both companies should have considered next best alternatives. At the time of the merger, management of the companies stated that a key driver behind the merger was a desire to put Time-Warner media properties on the Web. In retrospect, it is obvious that Time-Warner could have accomplished this objective much more easily and at significantly lower costs to its shareholders (even though its past efforts at putting its media on the Web had been expensive failures) by means other than merging with AOL. The results of the AOL Time-Warner deal are not an exception; studies have shown that most acquisitions are financial failures measured by the returns to shareholders of the acquiring company.

The shareholders of Daimler-Benz should have asked this question when asked to approve the company's merger with Chrysler. Because of the size of the two companies and their different products, cultures, and business models, shareholders should have asked whether there was a better way for Daimler-Benz to achieve the benefits it hoped to get from the merger with Chrysler. As of the fall of 2003, many of the benefits had yet to result in financial returns to the company's shareholders. The Chrysler senior management team has since left, and Daimler-Benz managers run the operations. Only now, several years after the acquisition, are people from the two predecessor companies beginning to work well together. The stock price for the company tells the story of this deal: The market capitalization for the entire Daimler-Benz Corporation as of late 2003 was much lower than the combined value of the companies at the time of the merger.

IBM provides an example of how asking this question can yield positive results. Several years ago IBM embarked on a program to provide project management training for a large number of its employees. The cost of the program, when travel and time out of the office were included, was significant. Although on the surface it seemed that the company had to either reduce the number of employees that would get the training or cut back on the scope of the training, a third option, the next best alternative, was found. This alternative was distance learning, and the company then made an investment to put many of the project management courses online. The effort has been largely successful both in training and in savings. Even more important, IBM has seen the benefits of the training in employee productivity.

Do not be surprised if the answer you get to the question—"Is there another way?" is no. The answer might even include an element of derision from the proponents for the investment. Keep in mind that managers who questioned investments in e-commerce during the dot-com days were told that they just didn't "get it." This might or might not have been true, but whatever the situation, it is your job to question the proponents and seek alternatives. Accept the statement that you "don't get it" and ask the proponents to explain how you should "get it." The discussion will, hopefully, lead to better alternatives for the company's resources.

6. Assume That We Decide to Make This Investment. What Have We Learned from the Past? What Is in Our Lessons Learned Files?

All of us learn from our experiences, and it is always worthwhile to inquire what, if any, investments your organization has made in the past. Situations change, and you need to be especially careful to take what you hear with a grain of salt, because each person has his or her own perspective and memory of the event. You also need to be wary of people who suggest that the investment you are assessing won't work because "we tried it before and it didn't work." The worst thing that can happen after a company makes a bad investment is for it to become so conservative that investments for future growth are never made or made and then starved. The second worst thing that can happen after a failed investment is that people feel so risk averse that the company suffers from analysis paralysis, the desire to analyze investments to the degree where all uncertainty is eliminated, which is, of course, impossible.

Nevertheless, search for information on past investments. What worked, what did not, what happened, and why? Dig as deeply as you can, not just in your company, but throughout your industry. It might also be helpful to learn from the experiences of companies in other industries that embarked on similar investments. Evaluate the proposed investment against what you learn. For example, the experiences with ERP systems of similar size and complexity in other industries could be of value when you are evaluating a proposal to invest in one at your company.

Summary

The preliminary analysis will help you to eliminate quickly investments that are unlikely to be successful before you have devoted a great deal of resources and time to losing efforts. As many managers will tell you, success often results from the investments that you don't make, rather than the ones you do, because you don't have to waste time and resources on losing causes. You might also find it helpful to provide the preliminary analysis to the managers who develop proposals for your company's investments. Working through the preliminary analysis will allow proponents to develop better business cases for their investments, even before going into the detailed financial analyses. Think back to the trip you would be taking from Los Angeles to Boston; like a global positioning satellite (GPS) navigation system, the preliminary analysis will lead you to investments that will help you reach your destination.

Following the Roadmap

This section, which will appear through Chapter 7 illustrates how the Business Investment Roadmap can be used to help your company make successful business investment decisions that grow revenue, profits, and, ultimately, corporate value. Here's where you will get an opportunity to see the Business Investment Roadmap in action with a fictional company, Fresh Breeze, a composite of several consumer products companies that was introduced in the last chapter. You might want to skip these sections for now, and come back later to dig into the details. You can use the "Following the Roadmap" sections as templates when you are evaluating and executing investments at your company.

Introducing Fresh Breeze Corporation

Fresh Breeze is a Chicago-based manufacturer of detergents, personal cleaning products, and air fresheners. It has a number of manufacturing plants throughout the United States. It manufactures essentially all of its own products from commonly available raw materials. Fresh Breeze had approximately $1.1 billion in revenues in 2002, and it has been growing at about 5 percent per year in recent years, as shown in Table 3.1. The company's competitors include several multinational corporations and regional companies that produce house-brand products for supermarket chains and distributors. Fresh Breeze is slightly smaller in revenues than Dial Corp. (2002 revenues of $1.28 billion), significantly smaller than Colgate Palmolive (2002 revenues of $9.29 billion), and much smaller than Procter and Gamble (2003 revenues of $43.77 billion).

The company has three divisions: Personal Cleaning, Laundry Care, and Air Fresheners. About a third of its revenues come from each division. It sells its products throughout the United States through supermarkets, mass merchandisers, drug stores, and other outlets. The company's largest customer is Wal-Mart, which accounts for more than 20 percent of the company's sales, and its top 10 customers together make up approximately 50 percent of its business. Other major customers include IGA, a national distributor for independent supermarkets such as Costco, Target, CVS, Walgreens, and regional discount stores.

Table 3.1 Fresh Breeze Corporation, Net Sales and Sales Growth Percentages, 1999–2003

	1999	2000	2001	2002	2003
Net sales ($ in millions)	$953	$1,000	$1,050	$1,103	$1,158
Sales growth percentage		5%	5%	5%	5%

Preliminary Analysis of an Investment: Would You Like That Super-Sized?

Let's begin putting the Business Investment Roadmap into action with a hypothetical proposal from a marketing team. You'll quickly see that the proposal is not completely realistic, but it is excellent for providing a quick and simple example of using preliminary analysis.

Assume that a group of managers in the Laundry Care division at Fresh Breeze are considering a proposal, introduced by one of the marketing teams, to change the packaging size, presentation, and price points for its Summer Breeze line of laundry detergent. Under this proposal, the company would sell Summer Breeze in much larger, double-sized containers at about the same price as the regular Summer Breeze detergent bottles, a marketing position targeted at value-oriented shoppers. The regular-sized bottles would be phased out, which would leave the super-sized containers as well as smaller, convenience-sized packages.

Summer Breeze is currently priced to be competitive with other midtier major brands. The company realized many years ago that it could not compete for brand-oriented shoppers who almost automatically picked up their bottles of Tide or Wisk. Instead, the company sought customers who are value-oriented, those people who want a bargain, but are hesitant to try a completely unknown brand or label.

The marketing team backing the investment believes that offering customers more detergent at the same price as competitors' products will result in Fresh Breeze gaining market share from its competitors and, thus, increase revenues and profits. The larger containers will be particularly attractive at the discount stores and warehouse clubs.

Summer Breeze detergent currently claims 5 percent of the U.S. market for laundry detergent sold, and the analysis by the marketing team proposing the investment indicates that the new product size could double market share to 10 percent. According to the initial analysis, the super-sized detergent bottle will nearly double revenues by gaining market share from competitors.

How does this investment stack up in terms of the six preliminary analysis questions? Are the prospects as rosy as the proponents suggest? Let's apply the preliminary analysis, recognizing that some of the six questions might be more critical than others in the evaluation of this proposed investment.

1. What Will Be The Impact on the Company's Cash Flow If We Make This Investment and It Is Successful?

For the moment, assume that the marketing team is correct in that if the investment is successful it will increase market share of Summer Breeze detergent from 5 percent to perhaps, 10 percent. What would such a gain mean to cash flows?

First, this product extension is meant to take market share away from competitors, rather than to stimulate demand for additional product. Demand for laundry detergent is expected to continue its historical stable growth rate of about 2 percent, so the result of the increase in market share will be a larger piece of essentially the same pie. People don't wash clothes more often as the price of laundry detergent drops.

This is important because if the volume of detergent in a sales unit is doubled, consumers will need to make only half as many detergent purchases to meet their detergent needs, which remain relatively constant. (You can assume in this case that the larger bottle size will not cause consumers to use significantly more detergent per load, but consumer demand and behavior is an important consideration in any investment.) A consumer who purchased laundry detergent every two weeks would, with the new size, now purchase detergent about once a month.

At the same time, the new double-sized detergent bottles will be sold at about the same price as the original containers, so with the new packaging consumers will pay only half as much to meet their full detergent needs. If Fresh Breeze doubled its market share in this category, twice the number of customers would purchase Summer Breeze detergent, but revenues would remain the same, because Fresh Breeze would have cut its revenue per ounce by about half.

Finally, look at the effect of the new detergent bottle size on the cost of producing and selling (see Table 3.2). Assume that for the current product line, the detergent accounts for 20 percent (80 cents) of the total cost of the product, the packaging adds another 10 percent (40 cents), and distribution accounts for 10 percent (40 cents) of the costs for a unit, which averages a $4.00 wholesale price. Together these costs account for 40 percent of the wholesale selling price. Doubling the amount of detergent would increase the cost of the detergent by slightly less than two times, to $1.50 or 37.5 percent.

Table 3.2   Gross Margin Comparison of Regular-Sized Summer Breeze Detergent Bottle and Proposed Larger-Sized Summer Breeze Bottle

	Regular-Sized Bottle		**Proposed Larger-Sized Bottle**	
	Dollar Amount	Percentage of Price	Dollar Amount	Percentage of Price
Wholesale price	$4.00	100%	$4.00	100.00%
Detergent cost	$0.80	20%	$1.50	37.50%
Packaging cost	$0.40	10%	$0.65	16.25%
Distribution cost	$0.40	10%	$0.70	17.50%
Gross margin	$2.40	60%	$1.15	28.75%

Packaging costs would increase to 65 cents or 16.25 percent. Distribution costs would increase to 70 cents, or 17.5 percent. All told, this investment would increase these costs from 40 percent to 71.25 percent of sales. For a product with a low profit margin to begin with, this would be a disastrous move for the bottom line.

Finally, if Fresh Breeze pursues this investment, it might force its competitors to reduce their prices to adopt Fresh Breeze's strategy. The result of such a reaction would likely be that for all of its efforts, Fresh Breeze's increased market share would be short-lived. This is the bottom line: From the perspective of the effects on cash flow, this investment appears to be an unmitigated disaster.

2. Will This Investment Leverage Our Existing Competencies and Help to Create a Competitive Advantage?

The proposed investment would indeed leverage Fresh Breeze's existing competencies; the larger detergent bottles contain a detergent formula that has already stood the test of consumer acceptance in the market, it would be sold predominantly to the same types of consumers it already targets, and it would be sold through the same distribution channels. This is outweighed by other factors, however. Although on its face, this proposed investment would create a competitive advantage for Fresh Breeze, a closer examination shows that this is not the case. The company would potentially increase its market share solely on the basis of cutting its price. Fresh Breeze does not have any real competitive advantage that would allow it to lower its cost structure, especially relative to much larger competitors that obviously have lower production costs and a much larger volume over which to amortize R&D, marketing, and other general costs. The answer to this question, therefore, is "no."

3. Who Else Benefits, and How Much of the Benefits from the Investment Do They Get If We Make This Investment and It Is Successful?

Under the structure of this particular proposal, the only direct beneficiaries of this investment are likely to be consumers, who would not only benefit from the much lower price of Summer Breeze detergent, but from the general downward price pressure on competitive products that Fresh Breeze's actions would likely cause. (This assumes that the retailers do not raise the price on the larger bottles to gain higher margins.) Fresh Breeze, accordingly, does not stand to gain anything from the investment outlined in this proposal other than profitless gains in market share. Competitors are unlikely to profit from Fresh Breeze's actions in the near term; in the long term, it might weaken Fresh Breeze, which could indirectly benefit its competitors. The investment does not pass muster in this segment of the preliminary analysis, either.

4. What Is the Long-Term Commitment, If We Make This Investment and It Is Successful? Will We Need to Devote Cash to the Investment on an Operating Basis After the Initial Investment Is Made?

The up-front development costs for this investment are fairly minimal and mostly involve developing new packaging, adjusting the manufacturing equipment and costs associated with the fairly minor but notable differences in distribution and shelf space for the larger product. There would be some additional investment and long-term commitment in terms of shipping costs and infrastructure changes to handle the larger containers. Once the new product size is launched, it will require the same sort of operating support as other products. The company already has vast experience supporting laundry products, so the incremental operating costs, if any, associated with this investment would be unlikely to cause many surprises. What *should* be a concern, however, is that the analysis in question 1 showed that the costs associated with this investment will likely outweigh any benefits received from it indefinitely.

5. Assume We Want to Make This Investment, But Cannot. What Is the Next Best Alternative? Is There Anything We Can Do Differently That Gets Us Nearly the Same Benefits in Cash Flow Returns to the Company?

Especially given the distinctly negative impact this investment is expected to have on cash flows, there are likely to be innumerable other investments that are superior to the proposal currently being scrutinized across many different areas of operation and functions of the company. Even restricting the alternatives to investments in product extensions with the intent to increase market share profitably, the choices are still quite varied, considering the size of the company and the variety of products it manufactures. If the general idea of selling more Summer Breeze detergent has appeal to the managers, they should examine other ways to invest to grow corporate value.

Alternatively, the marketing team might consider placing a series of small "bets" (i.e., small investments) by offering a variety of new products and sizes to gauge interest (assuming that their retailers would support these efforts) and, then, invest more resources in the products that have the greatest initial success. More broadly, Fresh Breeze should consider this and similar proposals in the context of its overall investments and prioritize investments according to their potential and likely impact on incremental cash flows.

6. Assume That We Decide to Make This Investment. What Have We Learned from the Past? What Is in Our Lessons Learned Files?

Given its long operating history and the array of products it offers, Fresh Breeze has a large store of experience in launching product extensions on which it should draw. Managers should look for similar investments the company has made in the past, evaluate their relative success or failure, and try to determine what caused each success or failure. The managers should also draw on the experiences of other companies that sell cleaning products in the same and similar distribution channels. By incorporating these lessons learned, the company's managers might be able to restructure the investment to provide more attractive returns and, ultimately, grow corporate value.

Preliminary Analysis Results

Taking the time to apply the first element of the Roadmap, preliminary analysis, should indicate to Fresh Breeze management in no uncertain terms that they should not make this investment, at least not in its current form. The first question, about the cash flows the investment is likely to generate, was both the critical question and the showstopper. Decisions on other investments with cash flow prospects that look better might hinge on the answers to the other questions in the preliminary analysis. Thus, you need to repeat the process for every investment you consider.

4

BUSINESS IMPACT ANALYSIS

"First Things First"

Steven Covey, Roger Merrill, and Rebecca Merrill

Silver Bullets and Golden Nuggets

Andy Grove, a founder and the former CEO of Intel, one of the world's most successful companies, wrote a business best-seller several years ago entitled *Only the Paranoid Survive*.[1] In his book, Grove asks managers this question: "If you could aim a 'silver bullet' at a single company and eliminate that company as a competitor, who would that company be?" This question helps managers identify their

---

1. Andrew S. Grove, *Only the Paranoid Survive: How to Exploit the Crisis Points That Challenge Every Company* (New York: Doubleday, 1999).

key competitors, which is an important step in developing corporate strategies. Obviously, the silver bullet question is theoretical, but it can help you determine who your primary competitors are and develop action plans to help your company increase its value. Try it among your colleagues, and one of the more surprising findings might be the lack of consensus among the group in determining who your company's primary competitor is.

Think about growth opportunities in your business in the same way that Andy Grove defined competitors. Instead of silver bullets, growth opportunities are built on your golden nuggets, the areas of your business that provide the greatest return for your incremental investments. Identifying your golden nuggets is the first step in determining where your company will get the greatest bang for its buck when you make investment decisions. In the same way that you posed the silver bullet question, ask your colleagues what they consider to be the golden nuggets in your company.

Determining your golden nuggets and developing strategies to exploit them is usually much easier said than done. In his best-selling book, *Good to Great*, Jim Collins describes leading companies as gaining insight into what he calls their "economic engine." He notes that, "The central point is that each good-to-great company attained a deep understanding of the key drivers of its economic engine and built its system in accordance with this understanding."[2] Collins then goes on to describe how companies adopt a single key ratio, what he calls a *denominator*, to gain an understanding of their economic models.

Collins is absolutely correct, but the *key* is in determining what he labels the denominator, or golden nugget. There might be several golden nuggets at your company. They usually are obvious in

---

2. Jim Collins, *Good to Great: Why Some Companies Make the Leap and Others Don't* (New York: Harper Business), pp. 104–106.

hindsight, but often difficult to determine without a thorough analysis. This chapter shows you how to find the golden nuggets in your company. Once you have identified them, you can use them to evaluate potential investment opportunities.

Figure 4.1 provides an overview of this step within the Business Investment Roadmap. As shown in the illustration, after you have completed the preliminary analysis, you assess the investment in the context of total returns. In this way you can determine whether the investment is more likely to enhance and grow corporate value by building and expanding your golden nuggets, or reduce the potential for growing value. This process covers two steps that:

- Identify the ways in which you can grow value in your company through an assessment of how to increase incremental cash flows.

- Determine which factors or "value drivers" are the golden nuggets—the value drivers from which your company will get the biggest bang for its buck through increased incremental cash flows. If you know what they are, you can turn your golden nuggets into full-fledged treasures.

Before getting into the details, please note that once you identify your golden nuggets, you will need to revisit your analysis periodically to make sure that they have not changed. What worked in the past or what looks like it will work in the future, from today's viewpoint will probably not remain static because of constantly changing macroeconomics and industry dynamics. This can turn your golden nuggets into fool's gold.

There are many companies who have fallen victim to this fool's gold. One dramatic example is Digital Equipment Corporation (DEC). At one time, DEC was the second largest computer company in the world, setting the standards for a quality-of-life working environment. The founder, Ken Olsen, was a brilliant scientist with a vision to create midrange computers to compete with IBM's main-

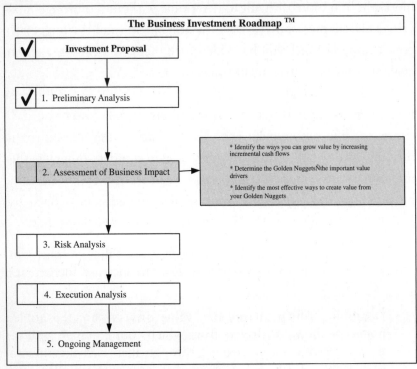

Figure 4.1   Decision Route: Business Impact

frame computers. Unfortunately for its employees and shareholders, DEC stumbled badly in the 1980s, and it eventually was acquired by Compaq (which has itself since been acquired by HP).

One of the major factors behind DEC's fall from grace was management's decision that the company's golden nugget in the future would be the mainframe business. DEC had experienced a great deal of erosion in its customer base as companies grew from DEC computers to IBM mainframes. As a response, the company reportedly devoted more than $1 billion to developing its own mainframe. In the meantime, however, the industry experienced a great deal of change and upheaval, brought about in part by the emergence of microprocessors, distributed computing, and the downward price pressures on computing power. The DEC mainframe was never successful—it was fool's gold—and the company missed out on the PC opportunity. This cautionary tale should keep you mining for your golden nuggets and watching out for fool's gold.

Cash Flow: The Critical Value Driver

Cash is king, and there is no one else in the royal court. The only ultimate return from any investment must be cash, and cash flow is an excellent proxy for creating value because cash is how you get your returns. Nearly every investment should be evaluated in terms of its impact on incremental cash flows. Even human-resource-related investments, in training and development for example, need to be assessed in terms of the cash flows from the improved worker productivity the training and development is expected to produce. If you cannot determine the impact on incremental cash flows from an investment, you really shouldn't go any further with the investment.

Warren Buffet, one of the world's wealthiest men and considered by many to be its most astute investor, considers free cash flow to be a key element when valuing a company. Under Buffet's analysis, the best companies in which to invest are those with significant free cash flows relative to investments. For Buffet, the ideal business might be one where the only investment is a mailbox to collect checks and a bank account for electronic transfers and depositing checks. (You, of course, need the golden nuggets to generate the cash.)

Companies have three primary ways of generating cash flow:

1. grow revenue

2. cut costs

3. improve productivity

Grow Revenue

One of the best ways to increase cash flows is to grow revenue. This assumes, of course, that costs remain at the same level relative to sales or decrease. There are four ways to grow revenue, and some companies use combinations of all four:

1. raise prices

2. sell new products and services

3. change your product mix

4. exploit existing assets

   Raise Prices: Companies often grow revenue by simply raising their prices. For example, the Boston Red Sox, perennial heartbreakers for their fans, play in Fenway Park, the oldest and smallest baseball stadium in the major leagues. Although the team already has the highest average ticket prices in professional baseball, fans in New England have come to expect an increase in Red Sox ticket prices every year with the same dependability as the annual fall foliage season and the collapse of the Sox.

   Raising prices to grow revenue can be a dangerous tactic for many companies. Unlike the Boston Red Sox, most companies do have a lot of competition, and an increase in prices can result in customer defections and fewer purchases by the customers that remain. At some point, an increase in prices will lead to a decline in revenue, as the revenues lost from customers that desert the company for less expensive alternatives outweigh the revenue gains from price increases. Consider the U.S. Postal Service, an organization that faces tremendous challenges as it appears stuck in the cycle of increasing prices and losing customers. Due to regular postage increases, particularly for business and "junk mail," the Postal Service has been losing customers. The combination of losing customers and the dampening impact of technology on mail volume (because of e-mails, greeting cards via e-mail, contracts with digital signatures, and other innovations) has resulted in declining revenues. In reaction, the Postal Service management raises prices to increase revenues, but the net effect is the loss of even more customers and lower mail volumes. The only business that the Postal Service is sure to keep, rural mail delivery, is a business that most of its competitors don't want.

Consider the nation's airlines, which at times seem to do their best to alienate their best and most profitable customers, business travelers. Many of the major carriers take advantage of business travelers by charging extraordinarily high fares as compared with the fares charged to leisure travelers. The pricing strategy of the major carriers has caused many business travelers to find alternatives, including teleconferencing and driving to cities serviced by discount carriers like Southwest ATA and Jet Blue to take advantage of the lower fares. The net effect is that the airlines are stuck with excess seats and have to reduce capacity, as most of the carriers have done during the recession.

Sell New Products and Services: There are other ways that companies can grow revenue. Continuing with the Red Sox example, the team could add seats to Fenway Park (which they have done, even putting seats in above the Green Monster, the wall in left field) or increase attendance at games by fielding a better team. The Red Sox have less maneuverability on the second option because they already sell out most of their games, but most businesses with a fixed number of seats do not enjoy such consistent sellouts. Similarly, if you follow the automobile industry, you might be familiar with BMW's strategy of adding a starter line of cars, the 1 Series, to grow revenue and increase customer loyalty. Both the Red Sox and BMW are growing revenue by adding new products. Consider the cookie section in the supermarket aisle, where Nabisco has added a wide range of Oreo cookies in different sizes and with different fillings and coatings.

Unfortunately, selling new products and services is usually easier said than done. Most businesses are extremely competitive, and the challenge of meeting competition on a day-to-day basis often outweighs the need to work on the development of new products and services. In effect, you need to sell new products and services just to stay even as your existing products and services are subjected to shortening market cycles and competitive threats. Consider again your local supermarket shelves; thousands of new products are introduced every year, but there is only limited shelf space. The result is a constant battle among manufacturers, with new products introduced practically every day to compete with existing products. From the manufacturers' perspective, they are on a treadmill that requires them to go at ever-increasing speeds simply to stay in position, let alone get ahead. In this environment, it is no wonder that many consumer products companies introduce primarily product line extensions like Oreos in different sizes, rather than entirely new products.

The treadmill runs even faster in many other industries, for example, telecommunications. The life cycle of a cell phone used to be about two years; today companies like Motorola, Nokia, Sony, Samsung, and others now work in approximately six-month cycles. Formerly "hip" products rapidly age and become albatrosses sitting on shelves and in warehouses.

This treadmill phenomenon is not limited to the fashion or high-tech industries. In the automobile industry, a "hot car" might be sold by dealers at a premium; just a few months later they can only be sold through incentives like cash-back offers or reduced lease rates. The latest version of the Ford Thunderbird was extremely popular when it was released a couple of years ago. The car was very hard to get, and some dealers understandably got full list price plus more. As of fall 2003, however, the car was readily available at most Ford dealerships. Those that were sold have depreciated relatively quickly, and Ford has announced plans to "retire" the model.

Change Your Product Mix: It truly is a battle to sell new products and services. Facing this challenge, many managers seek to change their product mix, accepting the fact that cycle times are decreasing. Instead, they focus on those products and services that can produce higher revenues to replace products and services that produce lower revenues. Let's return to the Red Sox and Fenway Park. Facing the challenge of growing revenue with a relatively fixed number of seats (even after raising prices and expanding the total number of seats), the team could add special concierge services for people sitting in seats located in the lower deck, close to the field. The services could include fetching snacks and beverages so that fans do not have to leave their seats during the game, and section-specific restrooms so that certain customers do not have to wait in long lines. They would then raise the price of those seats, and the end result would be growth in the team's revenue through changes in the product mix (higher priced seats).

Open your wallet and take a look at your credit cards. At one time, most of us had just a few credit cards; today, we have many options with different prices and services. American Express has been particularly astute in changing its product mix in response to the changing credit card market. Where there was once the standard green American Express card, consumers can now get a Gold, Platinum, or even a Black card. The annual fee for the Black card is $2,500, a substantially higher fee than the $50 or so that the company charges for its standard card. The net effect is a change in the company's product mix, and higher revenue derived from certain customers. (American Express has also been able to grow its customer base in several card categories.) This is an example of how companies seek to change their product mix in response to the challenge of growing revenue in a mature market. In the household appliance business, manufacturers have bifurcated the market by developing high-end, expensive appliances (e.g., the Neptune washers and dryers from Maytag). Manufacturers for other products such as clothing, food, and automobiles are following a similar strategy.

Exploit Existing Assets: The fourth way to grow revenue is by exploiting your existing tangible and intangible assets. Your company might have assets (e.g., intellectual property) that can be licensed to other firms on a royalty basis that will yield more revenue to you. Texas Instruments, for example, derives a sizable portion of its revenue stream from licensing fees based on its patents. Many other companies have been successful in leveraging their brand names or reputation for quality in partnerships that produce revenue with minimal incremental investments. Visit a local toy store to see all of the products that have some association with Disney, and you might be prompted to think about ways that your company could grow revenue by exploiting existing assets.

There is also the potential for exploiting existing assets by selling additional services and products that build on what you have already sold to your customer base. This can include what is commonly called vertical integration; your company selling products and services that were, or could be provided by others to your customers. For example, many companies that provide first mortgages, including Countrywide Mortgage and Washington Mutual, have now entered the home equity, second mortgage, and debt consolidation businesses.

Alternatively, companies can exploit the asset of their customer base by obtaining products from others, rebranding the products, and selling the products to their customers. Dell Computer, for example, resells computer peripherals made by other companies.

IBM sold a personal digital assistant that was developed by Palm. HP has a product like the Apple iPod. The classic case of this approach for revenue growth and profits, however, is the fashion industry, where companies commonly put their label on and sell products that are designed and manufactured by others.

Table 4.1 gives a simple example of the four ways to increase revenues just discussed. Scenario A serves as the baseline for revenues, where the company sells 100 units each of two products, A and B. Product A sells for $10, Product B sells for $9, and both cost $5 per unit to produce. In the baseline scenario, total gross margin for both products combined is $900. Because this is the baseline for the analysis, the incremental value created is zero. For simplicity, the model assumes that gross margins become cash flows in their entirety. Scenario B shows the effect of raising the price of Product A by $1. Assuming costs remain the same, the new total gross margin for both products combined will be $1,000, or $4,100 in incremental value created. In Scenario C, the company adds a third product, Product C, and sells 100 units for $8 per unit, at a cost of $4 per unit. In this case, the total gross margin increases to $1,300, with $400 of incremental value created from this investment. In Scenario D, the company changes its product mix from 50:50 between Products A and B to 75:25 in favor of Product A. Total gross margin under this scenario is $1,100; the investment has created $200 in incremental revenue. Finally, in Scenario E, the company licenses the rights to produce and sell Product C to another company, in exchange for 10 percent of revenues. The business that is licensing Product C sells 1,000 units, which in turn provides the company with $800 in revenues. Gross margins in this scenario are $1,800, an incremental value increase of $900.

The example in Table 4.1 is just that, an example, to show you how the four types of investments in growth work; you will need to consider every investment on its own merits.

Table 4.1   Four Ways to Increase Revenues

Four Ways to Increase Revenues					
Scenario A. Baseline Revenues					
	Units	Product	@	Unit $	Total
Sales	100	A	@	$10.00	$1,000.00
Costs	100	A	@	$5.00	$500.00
Gross Margin	100	A	@	$5.00	$500.00
Sales	100	B	@	$9.00	$900.00
Costs	100	B	@	$5.00	$500.00
Gross Margin	100	B	@	$4.00	$400.00
				Total Gross Margin	$900.00
				Incremental Value Created	$0.00
Scenario B. Raise Prices					
Raise Prices of Product A by $1.00, costs remain constant					
	Units	Product	@	Unit $	Total
Sales	100	A	@	$11.00	$1,100.00
Costs	100	A	@	$5.00	$500.00
Gross Margin	100	A	@	$6.00	$600.00
Sales	100	B	@	$9.00	$900.00
Costs	100	B	@	$5.00	$500.00
Gross Margin	100	B	@	$4.00	$400.00
				Total Gross Margin	$1,000.00
				Incremental Value Created	$100.00
Scenario C. Sell New Products					
Introduce Product C, Sell 100 units at $8.00, per unit costs $4.00					
	Units	Product	@	Unit $	Total
Sales	100	A	@	$10.00	$1,000.00
Costs	100	A	@	$5.00	$500.00
Gross Margin	100	A	@	$5.00	$500.00
Sales	100	B	@	$9.00	$900.00
Costs	100	B	@	$5.00	$500.00
Gross Margin	100	B	@	$4.00	$400.00
Sales	100	C	@	$8.00	$800.00
Costs	100	C	@	$4.00	$400.00
Gross Margin	100	C	@	$4.00	$400.00
				Total Gross Margin	$1,300.00
				Incremental Value Created	$400.00
Scenario D. Change Product Mix					
Change Product Mix of Product A and B from 50:50 to 75:25					
	Units	Product	@	Unit $	Total
Sales	150	A	@	$11.00	$1,650.00
Costs	150	A	@	$5.00	$750.00
Gross Margin	150	A	@	$6.00	$900.00
Sales	50	B	@	$9.00	$450.00
Costs	50	B	@	$5.00	$250.00
Gross Margin	50	B	@	$4.00	$200.00
				Total Gross Margin	$1,100.00
				Incremental Value Created	$200.00
Scenario E. Exploit Existing Assets					
License Rights to Product C for 10% of Revenues					
	Units	Product	@	Unit $	Total
Sales	100	A	@	$11.00	$1,100.00
Costs	100	A	@	$5.00	$500.00
Gross Margin	100	A	@	$6.00	$600.00
Sales	100	B	@	$9.00	$900.00
Costs	100	B	@	$5.00	$500.00
Gross Margin	100	B	@	$4.00	$400.00
Sales	1000	C	@	$8.00	$8,000.00
Royalties	1000	C	@	$0.80	$800.00
				Total Gross Margin	$1,800.00
				Incremental Value Created	$900.00

CHAPTER 4 • BUSINESS IMPACT ANALYSIS

Cut Costs

Another way for a company to achieve increased profits and resulting cash flows is to cut costs. If you have revenues of $1,000 and costs of $900, you get a pretax income of $100. If revenues are not growing, the only way that you can increase income is to reduce costs. If you lower costs to $850 in this example, you will generate pretax income of $150.

The primary cost for most manufacturing, distribution, and retail companies is the cost of goods sold (COGS). This is the cost incurred by the company to acquire the products or raw materials that are used to make the products. Going back to basic financial accounting (there is a review of accounting and finance in the Appendix), the top line on a company's income statement (see Table 4.2) is revenue. The second line is COGS. COGS is subtracted from revenue and the resulting number is called gross margin. You then subtract out expenses to determine income before taxes.

Table 4.2   Income Statement

Income Statement	2003	Percentage of Revenues
Revenues	$1,000	100.0%
Less cost of goods sold (COGS)	$400	40.0%
Gross margin	$600	60.0%
Less sales expenses	$110	11.0%
Less administrative expenses	$90	9.0%
Less general expenses	$100	10.0%
Operating margin	$300	30.0%
Less interest expense	$50	5.0%
Earnings before taxes	$250	25.0%
Less provision for income taxes	$80	8.0%
Net income	$170	17%

COGS relative to revenue and the resulting gross margin can tell us a lot about a company and its industry. Microsoft, one of the world's most profitable companies, typically has gross margins that exceed 80 percent. This was one of the issues raised by some members of the U.S. Congress, whose argument was that such high gross margins indicated that the company must have a monopoly. At the other extreme, companies in the wholesale distribution business are fortunate if their gross margins exceed 25 percent; the costs of the products they sell account for about 70 to 85 percent of their revenues. For supermarkets, the gross profit margins are generally even smaller. Of course, there are exceptions like Wegman's Food Markets, an industry leader, based in upstate New York, with stores in New York, Pennsylvania, New Jersey, and Virginia.

It is important to keep your COGS as low as possible, particularly in relation to your competitors. A company with lower COGS can pass those savings on to consumers in the form of lower prices or other benefits and gain a competitive advantage. Wal-Mart is a company known to be ruthless in managing all costs, particularly inventory costs. It has much lower COGS than most of its competitors. The company exploits this advantage by offering lower prices than department stores and, now that it is a major player in the grocery business, grocery stores. Wal-Mart achieves higher profits and cash flows than the industry, even with its lower prices for customers. The retail landscape is littered with companies that tried to compete with Wal-Mart but failed because of their higher operating costs.

Cutting COGS does not guarantee success, and it might not be a primary driver for increasing value at your company. Consider the restaurant business: If reducing COGS means a decrease in the quality of the ingredients purchased by a restaurant, the end result could be dissatisfied customers, loss of business, and a decline in value. Who would want to patronize a restaurant that promotes itself as buying the lowest priced ingredients? Similarly, you need to wonder how some restaurants, even fast-food establishments, can charge so little, given what it costs to buy the ingredients for their meals.

Operating Costs: Many companies seek to reduce operating costs in difficult economic periods to maintain profits or, in severe situations, simply to survive. Many of us are all too familiar with the refrains that we must "tighten our belts," "get lean and mean," or "get more efficient." It is true that like many of us who party and gain weight during the holiday season and then need to go on diets in the spring months, nearly all companies become inefficient during boom times. A changing economy forces rethinking and cutting back on costs. The downside to using primarily cost cutting to increase or even stabilize cash flows when revenues are declining or flat is that it becomes difficult to make investments for growth opportunities in the future.

Nevertheless, managers faced with difficult economic conditions must and do make cuts in operating costs so that cash flows can remain relatively stable. It is important to keep in mind that operating costs should and must be minimized whenever possible. Every missed opportunity to reduce operating costs is a missed chance for the company to increase cash flows available for new investments and to shareholders; it is an opportunity for the competition. In many industries, this means a race for efficiency, as companies seek to emulate best practices in their industry to reduce operating costs. Recently, this has meant a tremendous push for outsourcing on a global basis. Today, your call for satellite television service is likely to be answered by a representative in the Philippines. A call for technical support for an electronics product is likely to be answered by a representative in India or somewhere else in the world.

Other companies have sought to cut costs by having the customer do more of the work. When was the last time that you called FedEx versus using the Web to arrange a shipment? Consider, as well, how most of the airlines provide incentives to people who book flights online versus on the phone. The cost of handling the reservation online is significantly less than if an agent handles your call and books the flight for you. Similarly, if you have not traveled recently, try calling one of the major airlines. You likely will be greeted by a voice response system that will seek information from you so that the agent who eventually answers your call already has your information on the screen and can handle the call more quickly and efficiently. Southwest Airlines, the most consistently profitable airline, has the highest Web usage, as measured by the number of tickets booked over the Web, of any airline. Southwest is clearly efficient and good at cutting operating costs so that there is more money available to shareholders.

Although cutting operating costs is critical to competing successfully, the broader question is whether the investment needed to reduce operating costs is the best way to spend the company's money. The Southwest Airlines example shows that there can be a good bang for the buck, but in other industries the returns might not be so positive, or might, in fact, result in the loss of corporate value. Buying an airline ticket from Southwest when you know what you are getting is quite different than buying clothing online, as many clothing retailers discovered after spending enormous sums to create Web sites for selling their products online. Product returns from customers were much higher than returns from sales made via catalogs or at retail stores.

Improve Productivity

Another way that companies can increase incremental cash flows is to become more productive. Although productivity gains are often linked with cuts in operating costs, the reality is companies create productivity gains by using their existing resources more efficiently. Consider a company's assets as they appear on the balance sheet, as shown in Table 4.3.

Think about inventory—the products available for sale—and assume that this company is able to "turn" its inventory four times a year. In other words, on average, inventory is sold to customers, replaced, and sold again four times a year. Let's assume that after an investment in inventory management software, the company is able to increase its inventory turnover to six times a year by carrying products that are more popular and eliminating products that just sit on the shelves. The company becomes more efficient at managing its inventory, and will create value from this new efficiency.

One of the most frequently cited examples of a company that is extraordinary at managing its inventory is Dell Computer. Dell buys inventory for making computers on a seven-day cycle. The company rarely gets stuck with obsolete inventory, and it does not have to spend much on warehousing raw materials. Compared with its competitors, a major portion of Dell's profits come not from selling computers, but from the company's ability to manage its inventory and its resultant reduction in inventory investment.

Table 4.3 Assets on the Balance Sheet

Balance Sheet	December 31, 2003	Percentage of Total Assets
Current assets		
Cash and marketable securities	$60	6.0%
Accounts receivable	$200	20.0%
Inventory	$240	24.0%
Total current assets	$500	50.0%
Property plant and equipment	$600	60.0%
Less accumulated depreciation	$100	10.0%
Net property and equipment	$500	50.0%
Total assets	$1,000	100.0%

The same logic applies for the management of accounts receivable, the money owed to a company by customers who made prior purchases on credit. A company that collects money from its customers faster is using its accounts receivable assets more efficiently. Collecting accounts receivable sooner is so important that many companies have invested in collections systems. All of these systems provide the basic and simple functionality of contacting and dunning customers for money. The advanced systems provide the functionality that enables companies to learn about and remedy the reasons behind the slow payments, for example, overpromises by the sales staff.

Efficient management of inventory and accounts receivable is critical to many companies. In fact, one of the ways that companies (and managers) are evaluated is on how fast they turn inventory and accounts receivable compared to other companies in their industries. Investments that enable companies to increase inventory and accounts receivable turnover can often provide good bang for the buck.

Fixed Assets: Most companies also have significant investments in fixed assets—buildings, plant, and equipment—the infrastructure needed to conduct business. Here again, as with inventory and accounts receivable, there are opportunities for productivity gains that will increase profits. For example, a company that uses its space more efficiently will have a lower cost of doing business compared to its competitors. Similarly, a company that is able to operate its facilities on a 24/7 basis is likely to be more efficient than one that is on a five-day per week, 8 to 6 schedule.

Although it does not appear on the balance sheet, you need to think about more efficient utilization of your intangible assets, particularly human capital. Using the simple metric of revenue per employee or profits per employee, it is immediately obvious in most industries that some companies are more efficient in their use of people. Obviously, there are a variety of factors behind differences in employee effectiveness; the key issue here is determining if opening the corporate checkbook for HRM activities is the best way to invest compared to the alternatives.

Operational Levers

It is useful to think of increasing sales, reducing costs, and increasing efficiency as operational levers with which you can create value. Investments in these three areas flow through your company's operations differently; you can see the effects cascade through your financial statements over time. All of these types of investments only create value when certain conditions and requirements are met. For example, in an investment to increase revenue, the value of the incremental sales gained must be greater than the incremental costs incurred. In addition, just as "pushing" the sales lever toward increased sales can create cash flow, "pulling" it the other way can erode cash position. The cost and efficiency levers can also work in both directions, so you must be careful to make sure you move them in the right direction. You must also compare the benefits of an investment with its costs. In your analysis of value drivers, the golden nuggets, you are first concerned with the areas of investments where you can potentially create the most value, assuming that the other factors are consistent with a successful investment.

Table 4.4 shows the cascading effect of an investment to increase sales, moving from sales through costs, gross margin, net income, and incremental cash flows. Whether an increase in sales produces incremental cash flows depends on the relationship of incremental sales to incremental costs. Scenarios A through D illustrate this point. In Scenario A, the incremental sales come at a loss, because incremental costs are greater than the incremental revenues gained by the investment. Cost of sales as a percentage of sales increases, which drives down gross margin percentage and net income percentage. It has the ultimate effect of reducing operating cash flows, as the company incurs a loss with each new sale.

In Scenario B, the increased sales are at diminishing returns because the costs of the incremental sales are greater than the original costs of sales. As a result, cost as a percentage of sales increases, and gross margin percentage and net income percentage decrease. In this case, however, the cash flow effect is positive because the additional sales do provide a positive, although diminishing return.

Table 4.4   Investment to Increase Revenues

	A. Increased Sales at a Loss	B. Increased Sales, Diminishing Returns	C. Increased Sales With No Cost Efficiencies	D. Increased Sales With Cost Efficiencies
Sales	Increase	Increase	Increase	Increase
Cost% of sales	Increase	Increase	Constant	Decrease
Gross margin% of sales	Decrease	Decrease	Constant	Increase
Net income% of sales	Decrease, net loss on incremental sales	Decrease	Constant	Increase
Incremental cash flows	Negative	Positive	Positive	Positive
Cash flow trends	Every incremental sale for a loss	Increase at a decreasing rate	Increase at a constant rate	Increase at an increasing rate

Scenario C assumes that sales increase with no change in the underlying cost, gross margin, or net income percentages. In other words, the company does not achieve lower operating costs through increased sales volumes. In this case, each incremental sale increases incremental cash flows by the same margin amount.

Finally, Scenario D illustrates the effect of increasing sales where the increase in sales also reduces costs through operational efficiency; in this case, incremental cash flows increase at an increasing rate as sales increase. It should be clear that Scenario D provides the greatest potential return, followed by Scenarios C and B. Scenario A would erode the company's value.

Table 4.5 illustrates the effect of an investment to decrease costs on costs, gross margin and net income percentages, and incremental cash flows. The benefits of a cost reduction investment depend on whether sales decrease, remain constant, or increase in conjunction with the reduction in costs.

Scenario A depicts an investment in reducing costs that results in a decrease in sales. The effect on the cost percentage of sales, the

Table 4.5 Investment to Decrease Costs

	A. Sales Decrease	B. Sales Constant	C. Sales Increase
Cost% of sales	Decrease, unless it interferes with operating efficiency	Decrease	Decrease
Gross margin% of sales	Increase, unless it interferes with operating efficiency	Increase	Increase
New income% of sales	Increase, unless it interferes with operating efficiency	Increase	Increase
Incremental cash flow	Depends on relative size of cost savings and sales decrease	Positive	Positive

gross margin percentage of sales, and the net income percentage of sales depends on the degree to which sales are decreased. If the decrease in sales interferes with operating efficiency (because fixed costs are distributed over fewer units sold), the effect of the cost reduction might be negated to the extent of the interference. Therefore, Scenario A might or might not produce positive incremental cash flows, depending on the relationship of the cost savings to the reduction in sales.

In Scenario B, sales remain constant, such that the cost savings and resultant improvements in gross margin and net income amount to the percentage of sales that are saved through the investment in cost savings. Everything else being equal, Scenario B produces positive incremental cash flows, depending on the percentage of cost savings and the total sales.

Scenario C involves a reduction in costs and a concurrent increase in sales. Obviously, this is the type of cost reduction investment that produces the highest returns; the investment creates savings from existing sales levels, and, in addition, applies those savings to the incremental sales.

The third type of investment, in increased productivity, is a combination of an increase in revenues and a reduction in costs. It allows a company either to produce more at a given level of input (costs), or to produce the same amount at a lower cost. Table 4.6 illustrates the effect of an investment in increased productivity, assuming an increase in sales. Costs remain constant; thus, for a given level of costs, the company enjoys an increase in sales. The cost percentage of sales declines, along with the concurrent increase in gross margin percentage and net income percentage. These investments produce positive incremental cash flows.

Table 4.6 Investment in Increased Productivity

Sales	Increase
Costs	Constant
Cost% of sales	Decrease
Gross margin% of sales	Increase
Net income% of sales	Increase
Incremental cash flows	Positive

Determining the Best Bang for the Buck

To determine which value drivers are your golden nuggets, you should think about what would happen if sales, gross margins, and operating margins changed. An increase in sales should increase value, whereas a decrease in costs or expenses should also increase value. However, you must go further than this in your analysis. In reality, the increase in sales would most likely result in creating more value than is shown. The increased sales volume would decrease COGS percentage, because your fixed costs (the costs of keeping the business operating no matter what your level of sales) would be spread over the additional sales.

There are two other important factors to keep in mind: First, you must evaluate changes in sales growth rate and COGS percentage in the context of what is realistic for your company, given its own unique situation. If your company already enjoys low COGS due to some comparative advantage relative to your competitors, it will be harder to institute a further reduction in COGS than if your company has high costs of sales. If you are in the oil exploration and recovery business, your cost of sales would be much lower in some areas, say, the Middle East where the cost is less than $2 per barrel, versus the North Sea where it is much greater. Second, the interactions among sales growth, COGS, and value creation are all interrelated and should be considered as such. This caveat is important to keep in mind in your own analysis.

Listen to Your Financial Statements and the Business Climate

Generally speaking, you will achieve a greater bang for the buck with investments that grow sales versus investments to reduce costs and increase productivity. This assumes, however, that the investments are successful, a key issue throughout this book. This does not mean that you should ignore the expense side of the income statement. Rather, you should "listen" to what your income statement and the overall business climate in your industry are telling you. If you recognize and focus on the key value drivers for incremental cash flows in your company, you are less likely to get caught up on efforts that promise high financial returns but end up creating only minimal returns to your shareholders.

It is not enough simply to say that you are going to increase sales or reduce costs. You must think about the exact mechanism you plan to use. For example, you can increase sales by introducing new products, increasing your prices, lowering your prices, or changing your product mix. Although each approach can increase revenues, they all have different effects on cash flow and value creation for your company. Some sales increases might affect costs as well, which could give you less bang for the buck.

Similarly, you can reduce costs in a number of different ways: improving efficiency, utilizing capacity more efficiently, or using less expensive raw materials. Each of these strategies will have a different effect on cash flow and value creation. You must drill down into your investment plan to determine the value that your investment is likely to create.

To illustrate how to determine the best bang for the buck, let's think in more detail about sales growth. Increases in sales can create value for your company in two ways. First, the increased sales themselves create value. Second, they create value through improved operating margins. Whether or not sales growth improves operating margins depends on the nature of the sales increase and on the effects of those increased sales on your cost structure. For example, if you increase sales by $1 million, but spend $1.1 million to do so, you have eroded the value of your company, rather than increased it.

Sales are equal to units sold at particular unit prices, totaled across each product type and price point. Increased sales can result from increases in units sold or unit price, a change in the product mix (a change in volume of different products relative to each other), or a combination of these changes. It is not hard to see how increasing sales volume increases sales growth rate. If the cost structure remains the same or improves, you can increase value by selling more units. By the same token, if you increase prices while maintaining the same cost structure, you can increase profitability. These factors can influence both the sales growth rate and COGS.

Product Mix

The effect of changes in the product mix (i.e., selling different products) is a little more complex. Consider the automobile business for a moment and, specifically, the Daimler-Benz acquisition of Chrysler, an example discussed earlier. One of the justifications for the deal according to stories in the popular press was that the combined companies would have higher sales volumes, greater economies of scale, and, accordingly, lower COGS. After the deal closed, Daimler-Chrysler clearly had much greater sales volume, given the combination of Daimler-Benz and

Chrysler. This increased volume, however, came with a major shift in the company's product mix. The average sales price per car was lower, not unexpected given that the product line now included midmarket cars like Chrysler minivans and entry-market cars like the Chrysler Neon with a suggested retail price of less than $12,000. The company has also found that there have not been very many opportunities to leverage the higher sales volumes into reduced COGS. Who wants to be reminded that their new Mercedes-Benz has Chrysler parts and engineering?

In contrast, the product mix became richer for Metropolitan Insurance when the company acquired The New England, a well-known insurance company based in Boston. The New England's product mix and customer base were much "richer" than Metropolitan's, although Metropolitan was a bigger and more profitable company overall. Consider, as well, the acquisition of US Trust by Charles Schwab. The US Trust customers tended to have much larger portfolios and were "richer" as compared with the Schwab customers.

Although these product mix changes in the automobile and financial services industries were from acquisitions, many companies change their product mix by changing their own products, rather than by acquiring another company. DuPont, for example, has been able to change its product mix dramatically from feedstock chemicals to higher-value products and related services.

The Impact of Sales Changes on Capacity Utilization

Increases in sales can sometimes lower operating costs per unit produced. For example, businesses must invest in plant, equipment, and land, or product development to generate sales later on. These investments end up on the income statement either as depreciation or expenses. Depending on how they are classified, these investments can temporarily lower operating margins. The sales growth that occurs later as a result of these investments increases operating margins because the investments in plant and equipment or product development are not constant expenditures. This margin boost is referred to as *operating leverage,* and it leads to lower operating costs per unit produced. Simply assuming that efficiencies resulting from increased volumes will fall to the bottom line is incorrect; there must be sufficient demand in the marketplace for your products and services so that you will not suffer any price erosion or reduction in the perceived value of your products and services.

For sales to produce value, they must not only produce revenues, but net income and cash flows as well. In the extreme case, if the cost of the additional sales is more than the benefit you receive from those sales, you have a situation where your company loses value with each sale. This extreme case illustrates the importance of looking at all value drivers to see where you can make the most difference to the value of your company, rather than automatically focusing on increasing sales. Your industry and the specifics of your company's position in the market might also help dictate the best path to value.

Summary

The second element in the Business Investment Roadmap is designed to assess an investment's impact on creating value for your business by determining the golden nuggets—the areas of your business that can provide the greatest bang for the buck—and investing to make these golden nuggets even more valuable. Companies can generate incremental cash flow by increasing revenue, reducing operating costs, particularly the COGS, and by becoming more efficient in utilizing their assets. Increased revenue is usually the most fruitful way to grow value, followed by reducing costs through greater efficiencies. Simply cutting operational costs does not usually have a positive long-run impact on value creation.

The first step in assessing the business impact of an investment is to determine the baseline values for the value drivers of your business. You can use this baseline to identify the golden nuggets as well as to estimate the impact of an investment on value by comparing it to the baseline. Once you understand the important value drivers for your business, you have a number of different alternatives for driving these values to increase these incremental cash flows.

Following the Roadmap

Let's apply the business impact element of the Business Investment Roadmap by walking through the financial statements for Fresh Breeze. This process will provide some perspective on what you need to do to determine your company's best investment opportunities, or the golden nuggets.

From Table 4.7, you can see that sales at Fresh Breeze have been growing at 5 percent per year, and that COGS and Sales General and Administrative expenses have remained steady as a percentage of sales. Fresh Breeze has several investment alternatives for creating incremental cash flows; it can invest to increase sales, reduce costs, or improve productivity.

To determine the effect of an increase in sales on value at the company, consider the 5 percent sales growth rate. If you think of the 5 percent increase in sales from 2002 to 2003 as an investment that increases sales by 5 percent, you can see that gross margin

Table 4.7 Fresh Breeze Corporation Sales, COGS, Gross Margin, and SG&A, 2002 and 2003

	2002	% of Sales	2003	% of Sales
Sales growth rate	5%			
Sales (%Billions)	$1,103	100%	$1,158	100%
COGS	$482	44%	$506	44%
Gross Margin	$621	56%	$652	56%
SG&A	$386	35%	$405	35%

would increase by $652 – $621, or $31 million, for a growth rate of 5 percent that matches the sales growth rate, because costs remain at a constant percentage. Similarly, if Fresh Breeze reduced COGS by 5 percent from 2002 levels, while keeping sales constant, it would increase gross margin to $1,103 billion × 44% × 105% = $509 million, an increase of $17 million. The result would be identical if Fresh Breeze improved its production efficiency by 5 percent.

From this general analysis, it is clear that Fresh Breeze could create significant value by increasing sales, by decreasing costs, or by improving productivity. The question of which investment option the company should pursue depends on a number of factors, including the specific targets of the investments under consideration, and how realistic its assumptions are about moving its value drivers. Let's take a look at several investment alternatives Fresh Breeze is considering.

Increases in Revenues

The cash flow effect of increased revenues depends on the method used to increase sales and the costs related to those incremental sales, as discussed earlier in the chapter. The effectiveness of each method of increasing revenues depends largely on company and industry factors, in addition to execution-related issues.

For example, if Fresh Breeze increases the prices it charges wholesalers and retailers for its products, it could increase revenues. Nearly all of this additional revenue would filter down to income and cash flow. This assumes, of course, that costs remain constant. It also assumes that increasing price does not have a negative impact on sales levels. Unfortunately for Fresh Breeze, its industry is so competitive that any significant increase in prices would likely result in a significant decline in sales. Although the company could try and find an optimal price increase where the increased price would compensate for the loss in sales volume, this is not likely to be a particularly effective investment strategy for Fresh Breeze because of its fluid markets.

Fresh Breeze could also increase sales of its existing products. To do so, it would ultimately have to produce more products. If its manufacturing facilities have extra, currently unused capacity, it could ramp up production quite economically. On the other hand, assume that to enable the production increase, the company must build a new manufacturing facility. The factory would cost $80 million to build, which the company would pay for out of its cash reserves. After the plant goes online, the products manufactured there are expected to generate $40 million in revenues in Year 1, $60 million in Year 2, and $80 million in Years 3 and 4. Although net income in 2003 will be reduced because of the investment in a new manufacturing plant, in subsequent years, gross margins and net income will be higher if the plant is built and the products manufactured are sold without major discounts. Note the requirement that products manufactured are sold without major discounts.

Fresh Breeze has to also consider this investment in the context of whether it is feasible that it could sell the volume of products that are implicit in the benefit projections. If it has to cut its prices significantly, it would lose much of the projected benefits of this investment. In fact, this is a problem that many companies, including Proctor & Gamble and Campbell's (the soup company), have faced and sought to correct. Both of these companies had too much capacity and overproduced their products. Typically, the sales and marketing teams would provide "specials" in selected geographic areas or to customer groups. Unfortunately, for both companies, middlemen often diverted the products to other areas of the country, causing confusion in the retail channels. Additionally, both companies created situations in which it was difficult to maintain price points, because many buyers came to expect such "specials" regularly and planned their purchasing accordingly.

Fresh Breeze could also introduce new products to increase revenue. The feasibility of this approach depends on the cost to develop new products and bring them to market. If producing them involved an investment in a manufacturing facility similar to the one described in the example of increasing sales of existing products, the analysis would proceed similarly, with the added risk that it is an untested product.

Another alternative is for Fresh Breeze to change its product sales mix to create incremental cash flows. For example, in 2002 Fresh Breeze's sales were evenly split in terms of revenue among its personal cleaning, laundry care, and air freshener product lines, as shown in Table 4.8. Note that even though revenue is the same for all three product lines, unit volume varies considerably among the categories, as each has a different average unit price and cost. COGS percentage of sales for the company's air freshener products is 47.1 percent, which is lower than either personal cleaning at 58.4 percent or laundry care at 50.2 percent. This means, as shown in Table 4.8, that Fresh Breeze's air freshener segment is its most profitable product line in terms of percentage profit, followed by personal cleaning, and then laundry care products. Overall, Fresh Breeze has a COGS percentage of 51.9 percent.

Table 4.8   Fresh Breeze Corporation Sales Mix

	Sales Mix	Units	Unit Price	Unit Cost	Sales	COGS	Gross margin	COGS %
Personal Cleaning	33.3%	246	$1.49	$0.87	$367	$215	$152	58.4%
Laundry Care	33.3%	143	$2.56	$1.29	$368	$185	$183	50.2%
Air Fresheners	33.4%	159	$2.31	$1.09	$368	$172	$195	47.1%
Total	100.0%	548	$2.01	$1.04	$1,103	$572	$530	51.9%

Fresh Breeze's laundry care products have the highest per unit price ($2.56). The company generates more revenues per unit sale of products in this segment than with products in either of its other segments. Assuming that it is equally easy for the company to sell additional units of any of its products, efforts to increase sales of laundry care products would have a bigger impact on revenues than equivalent efforts in its other business segments. This would increase sales of laundry care products relative to the other segments, changing the product mix, and creating additional value. Given this data, if you were a senior member of the management team at Freeze Breeze, what would you initially focus on if given the mandate to create value? The obvious answer is to grow sales of laundry care products.

Now let's consider the effect of product mix on operating costs. Consider what would happen if Fresh Breeze's product mix was different, for example 40 percent for personal cleaning, 20 percent for laundry care, and 40 percent for air fresheners. Keeping total sales, unit price, and unit cost the same, Table 4.9 shows that gross margin increases by about $12 million for the same total sales, and, consequently, COGS percentage decreases to 43.4 percent.

Table 4.9 Fresh Breeze Corporation Sales Mix at 20:40:40 for Personal Cleaning, Laundry Care, and Air Fresheners

	Sales Mix	Units	Unit Price	Unit Cost	Sales	COGS	Gross margin	COGS %
Personal Cleaning	20%	148	$1.49	$0.87	$367	$129	$129	58.40%
Laundry Care	40%	172	$2.56	$1.29	$368	$222	$222	50.20%
Air Fresheners	40%	191	$2.31	$1.09	$368	$208	$208	47.10%
Total	100%	511	$2.16	$1.09	$1,103	$559	$545	50.6%

In reality, a company like Fresh Breeze probably could not change its product mix in the short run as significantly as shown in this example because of demand for certain products or access to markets large enough to support the increase in laundry care and air freshener sales. It would be easier for it to change its mix of products within its major product lines. The company also would be unlikely to change its product mix while maintaining constant sales. Instead, Fresh Breeze would try to increase sales of its more profitable product lines, not necessarily at the expense of existing sales of other products. It should be clear, however, that you can increase sales and profits by paying attention to and manipulating your product mix, focusing on your most profitable products. It sounds so simple, but as we will see in a later chapter, in reality, it can be a difficult task.

Investment to Reduce Costs

Senior management at Fresh Breeze is considering a proposal that will reduce the company's real estate costs by 10 percent by consolidating its office and distribution facilities. Although this management savings decision would result in incremental cash flows, the effect is slight because real estate does not account for a major portion of overall costs. The company likely should consider other investment areas first.

Fresh Breeze is also considering ways to reduce its purchasing costs, which currently are higher than the industry average. The company's actual pricing and ordering system is outdated. Pricing and ordering of raw materials is minimally automated, requiring a complicated series of phone calls and faxes with a large number of suppliers. This process, moreover, must continually be repeated because the company makes only short-term orders, rather than signing longer term contracts. These procedures were implemented initially because management believed that by shopping around for discrete orders among a large number of suppliers, it could ensure the best possible price for raw materials.

To address these problems, Fresh Breeze has decided to reduce its number of suppliers. Much like the major automobile manufacturers, instead of negotiating with many suppliers, the company plans to develop relationships with a smaller number of suppliers. It will purchase materials almost exclusively through these preferred relationships. The concentration of buying power enables Fresh Breeze to negotiate better prices from these suppliers, who, for obvious reasons, want to retain the business. In addition, it has contracts with these suppliers that ensure that it is receiving the lowest prices (often called most-favored nation status) for materials. This approach, the company determines, can save a net of 4 to 6 percent on its materials costs, which translates to approximately 2 percent of COGS. This represents a $10 million savings per year. Depending on the costs associated with this proposal, it appears that it might be worth management's attention to pursue. We'll return to Fresh Breeze and its investment opportunities in the next chapter.

5

RISK ANALYSIS

The revolutionary idea that defines the boundary between modern times and the past is the mastery of risk: the notion that the future is more than a whim of the gods and that men and women are not passive before nature.

Peter Bernstein, Against the Gods: The Remarkable Story of Risk

Although even the most well-planned and well-placed investments involve risk, managers often do not devote the time and attention needed to understand and mitigate the risks of their investments. ROI or payback analysis might promise tremendous returns, but risks that are overlooked or ignored can create problems or even cause the investment to fail. You can improve the success rate of your company's investments if you can identify, manage, and minimize the risks they face. Risk analysis is critical throughout the entire investment process, not just when you are evaluating whether to proceed with an investment.

To properly assess an investment, you need to be aware of all of its associated risks, and develop appropriate strategies for dealing with the most important risks. The most important risks do not mean *all* risks. In an ideal world, you would prepare for everything. In the real world of business, however, risk mitigation is costly and reduces the potential returns of an investment. If you try to prepare for every contingency, the added costs will quickly make the investment worth much less. This is why you focus on only the most important risks.

The Business Investment Roadmap lets you determine the important risks of every investment you undertake (see Figure 5.1). The approach to managing risk is intuitive: identify the risks you face, decide which of those risks are the most important, plan how to mitigate those selected risks, and incorporate these plans in your overall investment plans.

You don't need precise probabilities to figure out the most serious risks. At the end of the day, what matters the most is how well you execute your plans, not the probability your investment will go over budget by 5 percent is 20 or 21 percent. The four Business Investment Roadmap risk management steps as shown in Figure 5.1 are:

1. *Identify* and *categorize* the risks according to source, degree of uncertainty, likelihood of occurrence, and potential impact.

2. *Prioritize* the risks according to the profile you developed.

3. *Map* the risks relative to the returns, and classify the investment based on this relationship.

4. Develop risk mitigation plans to *minimize* each important risk, with more attention paid to the highest priority risks.

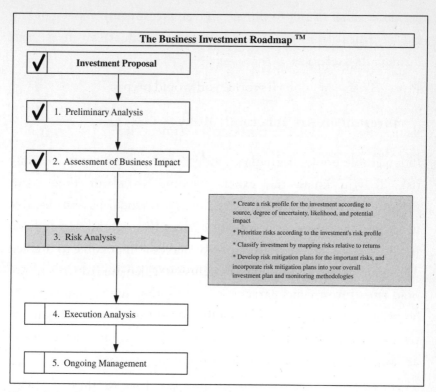

The Business Investment Roadmap ™

✓ **Investment Proposal**

✓ 1. Preliminary Analysis

✓ 2. Assessment of Business Impact

3. Risk Analysis

* Create a risk profile for the investment according to source, degree of uncertainty, likelihood, and potential impact

* Prioritize risks according to the investment's risk profile

* Classify investment by mapping risks relative to returns

* Develop risk mitigation plans for the important risks, and incorporate risk mitigation plans into your overall investment plan and monitoring methodologies

4. Execution Analysis

5. Ongoing Management

Figure 5.1 Business Investment Roadmap: Risk Analysis

What Is Risk?

The term *risk* has a wide range of meanings, depending on how it is being used. For people, risky behavior means engaging in activities likely to harm them. For corporate investments, risk is the likelihood that an investment will not achieve the expected result or return. The higher the risk, the greater the chance of failure. You need to strike a balance between risk and reward, because high-risk investments also usually have the potential for greater returns. In this way, you weigh potential risks against potential rewards to decide whether or not to pursue a given investment. Understanding risk is critical from the time you begin to evaluate an investment through its execution.

Investments Are Inherently Risky

Innumerable books, formulas, models, and experts try to quantify risk. If you knew the exact outcome ahead of time, your investments would succeed every time. You would have to be able to see into the future, or at least be extremely insightful, like Indiana Jones, because the very nature of risk makes it impossible to predict. The assumptions and estimates you use to calculate risks might not hold true. Investments carry risk because they use resources in the hopes of receiving benefits in the future. Although you can estimate the likelihood that something will happen, you cannot determine in advance whether it will happen or not.

Investments promise rewards precisely because they are risky. In the investing world, U.S. government securities are considered to be risk-free, but they really are not; there is no reward without risk. They carry the low, but possible risk that the government will default on them, and, appropriately, the offer of a low return or reward. As economists like to say, there is no free lunch.

Some industries treat risks differently than others; insurance companies, for example, focus on the probability of adverse events and the impact those events have. Using statistical models, insurance companies can predict, to a reasonable level of certainty, the number of claims they will have and can price their policies accordingly. This approach works best with yes or no questions, and it is of little use in evaluating most of the investment opportunities at most companies because of the large amount of empirical data required.

Investor Risk and the Limits of Portfolio Theory When Analyzing Business Investments: The investment community is interested in both the returns of investment and the predictability of those returns. For investors, low-risk investments have a known, stable, and likely return, whereas there is more uncertainty about the returns for high-risk investments. To reduce investment risk, most investors use portfolio theory to diversify their investments. The idea is that a diverse portfolio of investments limits the risk of the overall investment while maintaining the same expected returns. If you have your investments in different portfolios, the loss of one or two investments won't be significant in the entire portfolio.

The key to diversification is to choose investments with risks that vary independently of each other. There are three ways to do this: choose different kinds of securities (e.g., stocks and bonds) that have different risk characteristics and market drivers; choose securities in disparate industries where the risks and factors driving these industries are different; or choose securities with market drivers that work in opposite directions, called *hedging*. If the risks are independent of each other, the total risk of the portfolio will be less than the sum of its component risks. At the same time, the total expected return on the portfolio will be the same as the sum of each individual investment's return. Therefore, a properly diversified portfolio reduces risk for the same level of expected rewards. From the securities markets, portfolio theory has found its way into corporate management with some important differences. Diversification can indeed help your company reduce risk; diversifying your customer base, supplier base, or product offerings reduces the impact of losing a customer, losing a single supplier, or the disappointing sales of a particular product. No one wants to bet it all on one roll of the dice.

There are many risks you cannot diversify away when making corporate investments, in part because you usually face a wide array of interrelated risks. More important, investments within your company have profound implications on resource allocation, company operations, and strategic direction that make it impossible to treat them as part of an investment portfolio. Limits on budgets, time, and financial, physical, and human resources force you to narrow your focus and eliminate redundant efforts. Portfolio theory, premised on having multiple investments, is antithetical to this approach.

Another key difference between internal company investments and building a security portfolio is in the units of investment involved. If you had $1 million to invest in a portfolio of securities, you could diversify your investment over dozens or even hundreds of different securities because the unit of investment is the price of a share of stock. You can't diversify this way when making most investments at your company. If your company decided to invest in a major upgrade of its IT systems, you would not try to manage the risk of the investment through diversification. It would be absurd to make many small investments in multiple IT systems, with the expectation that some would ultimately work and others would fail. Instead, you need to choose a single system carefully and then focus attention on configuring and running it successfully.

Portfolio theory is directly applicable to other types of corporate investments as well. Consider, for example, R&D and new product development. Many companies have learned that it is better to have a series of relatively small ongoing efforts in R&D, rather than fewer efforts with large budgets. This approach enables companies to consider R&D efforts as options. Those efforts that make their milestones receive additional funding; those that do not are eliminated and new efforts are funded. This approach is particularly popular among pharmaceutical and high-technology companies. For example, pharmaceutical giant Merck has pioneered the use of options to fund and evaluate their R&D efforts. Genzyme, a leading biotech pharmaceutical company, reportedly uses a similar approach.

Four Ways to Evaluate Risks

There is no way to completely eliminate risk, but you can manage and reduce it if you understand and focus on the factors that contribute the most to the overall risk of your investment. The ability to identify and prioritize risk factors is a crucial skill in risk management. The Business Investment Roadmap makes this task easier because it provides a systematic way to evaluate risk factors using four criteria:

1. source

2. degree of uncertainty

3. probability

4. impact

By identifying and evaluating risks using these four classification schemes, you will create a risk factor profile for the investment under consideration. The risk profile of every investment opportunity is unique; thus, you need to go through this process each time you evaluate a new investment. The uniqueness of every investment means that you should also look for risk factors novel to a particular investment.

Sources of Risk

The first place to look for and categorize risks is by their source. A convenient way to look at the source of risks is whether they come from outside the company (external macro), come from within the company (business designs), or are specific to the investment under consideration (execution). Examining risk factors by their originating source is useful, not only in identifying all of the risks that an investment faces. Knowing the source also helps to determine how a given risk should be treated in the overall process. For example, because external macro risk factors are largely outside your company's control, they should be treated more like constraints on your investment strategy. Although your company has more control over business design risk factors, you need to make a decision whether to treat these as constraints or as risk factors. If you treat them as constraints, you are, in effect, investing based on your company's corporate strategy. If you treat them as risk factors, you change company strategy to meet a desired investment; this is possible, but it can be extremely dangerous.

Your company has the most flexibility in dealing with execution-related risk factors. Although you cannot eliminate these risks, you can change the plans and parameters of a particular investment so that its risk profile changes without attempting to change either wider economic forces or company strategy.

External Macro: Each investment your company makes is subject to the conditions and constraints of macroeconomic factors. These are defined by the market structure of your industry as well as the wider economy. These conditions and constraints are the same for every investment made by your company or any other company in your industry; they create the playing field on which you and your competitors all operate. Although the playing field in this sense is the same for all companies, the effects of these factors on investments vary by your company's position in that industry, and on the specific investment in question. Macro external risk factors include the following:

- *State of the overall economy, and the relationship of the industry to the overall economy.* Although this is an important factor, in most cases, it should be considered on an industry-wide rather than economy-wide basis. Different industries track against economic cycles differently, and business-focused versus consumer-focused industries also are affected differently. For example, McDonald's is affected differently by economic downturns than the Cheesecake Factory, although both companies are in the restaurant business. During a downturn, consumers might increase their purchases at inexpensive, fast-food restaurants and midprice restaurants could suffer accordingly.

- *Number of competitors in the industry.* The competitive environment for microprocessors, which has two main competitors, Intel and AMD, is much different than, say, that for the dry cleaning business, which consists mainly of thousands of small businesses. There is intense competition between Intel and AMD for their primary customers, which themselves are a small group of companies (e.g., Dell, IBM, HP, and Gateway).

- *Concentration of market share in the industry.* In the 12-volt automotive electronics industry, a niche industry, a few companies hold virtually the entire market share for car stereo head units. There are dozens of car speaker manufacturers, however, and the leading companies in this sector have much less dominance.

- *Degree of government regulation.* The profound effect government regulation can have on an industry is apparent in the example of the deregulation of airlines during the 1970s, and in the telecommunications industry from the 1990s to the present. In fact, the collapse of the telecom sector caused even greater losses for investors than the collapse of the dot-coms. For example, consider the impact of the Federal Communications Commission (FCC) rulings on the telecom industry and competitors to the regional Bell operating companies. In the late 1990s, there were literally hundreds of companies vying to provide local phone service in areas around the country. Most of these companies, called Competitive Local Exchange Carriers (CLEC), have since gone bankrupt, in part because of mismanagement, but also due to FCC policy changes that effectively changed the playing field.

- *Rate of industry growth and the growth rate of sectors within the industry.* Industries, and sectors within industries, behave differently depending on where they are in their industry life cycles. Consider, for example, the rapid growth in the past few years in the SUV model segment versus the sedan market in the auto industry. Manufacturers with product lines focused on sedans, like Saturn, have had to scramble to come out with an SUV model to compete.

- *Role of suppliers.* The role and relative power of suppliers in the overall value chain of an industry can have a strong effect on it. The next time you pull up at your local service station, think about the power and leverage the Organization of Petroleum Exporting Countries has in the marketplace for gasoline as well as in plastics and other petroleum-based industries.

- *Degree of capital intensity.* The degree of capital intensity influences a range of factors in an industry and, in effect, dictates how easily a new company can enter an industry, and how expensive it is to remain there. We might, at times, curse the airline industry for poor service and unreasonable pricing, but the significant capital intensity of the industry limits new competition.

- *Switching costs among products and services offered.* Transaction-based industries have very different risk characteristics than industries dominated by relationships with customers. Consider the risk profile for investments in building and maintaining relationships with customers using a cell phone versus selling people phone cards.

- *Life cycle and life span of products.* The life cycle and life span of products can have mendous effect on the economics and business model of an industry. Compare the fashion apparel industry, where products have very short life cycles and life spans, to the major appliance industry, where buying cycles and life cycles are much longer. Senior-level managers at the Gap have to think and act differently than senior-level managers at Maytag.

- *Substitutes available.* The availability and acceptability of substitutes affects the economics and business model of an industry; the fewer or less acceptable the substitutes available, the more customers are tied to the product. The risk profile for a company that has minimal leverage with customers because of easy customer exit options is quite different than one where customers have few alternatives. Consider the switch to cellular phone number portability in November 2003. Your cell phone number, which was a primary reason for staying with your vendor, no matter how bad the service, is no longer vendor-dependent. You can shop around to select the best vendor and keep your number. Churn rates, the percentage of the customer base that leaves, for the wireless companies will be much higher with number portability.

- *Complements available.* Compare the likely fate of software bolt-ons that work with SAP and Oracle versus bolt-ons for smaller players in the ERP space. As a customer, you have more risk with a smaller player because you have fewer options for bolt-ons that can leverage your investment in an ERP system.

These external macro risk factors apply consistently to all of the investments made by all of the companies in an industry. The success or failure of particular investments by companies within an industry depends mainly on the business design and execution of particular companies (the execution and mitigation of risk) as they apply within the framework of the overall business environment.

Execution Risk: The next chapter covers execution in more detail, but it is useful to consider some of the primary execution-related risks here as well. Execution-related risk factors commonly fall into the categories of duration, personnel experience, buy-in and corporate culture, research and data collection, documentation, alignment and benefits, and technology.

Duration: How long an investment takes can significantly impact risk. The general rule is the longer the time period, the greater the risk involved. Duration estimates are only as good as the assumptions you use in your calculations. Duration risk is so important that many companies deliberately cut investments into small chunks with relatively short duration periods, sometimes fewer than six months. For example, several studies have found that the probability of achieving success with an IT investment is inversely related to the time. Consider, for example, the problems Hershey had implementing SAP. Delays in that effort along with other ongoing issues helped to create a situation that cost the company well over nine figures in losses.

With a short duration and, accordingly, smaller deliverables and expectations, people are generally more focused, and there is less likelihood that a major risk will impact the investment. Put somewhat differently, longer is not better.

From the perspective of day-to-day activities, you are better off using more conservative (longer) estimates; if the investment works, given your worst-case scenario, it certainly will be a success if performance beats worst-case assumptions! Duration can be a big factor throughout the investment process, for example:

- The more time that passes between collecting the data and information with which you evaluate an investment and actually executing the investment, the greater the possibility that conditions will change such that they invalidate your analysis.

- Length of execution is often a good proxy for the complexity of an investment, especially in technology investments.

- Length of execution creates opportunities for proponents to make changes in scope and expectations.

- Payback time, or how long it takes to receive the benefits from an investment, is another critical risk factor. Shorter payback times mean less risk for the investment.

- Delay between decision and execution can be another factor. The more time that passes between the decision to make an investment and the start of its execution, the less you can rely on the analysis that prompted your decision in the first place.

Personnel Experience: The experience of the individuals and companies involved in an investment play a critical role in its risk. The more times you do something, the better you get at it. Consider, for example, the experiences with hernia repairs at Shouldice Hospital in Canada. Unlike most hospitals in North America, the primary focus at Shouldice is performing hernia repairs. The surgeons each perform between 600 and 800 hernia operations a year, more than most surgeons do in their professional lifetime. They not only perform more hernia operations a year, but they are able to do the operations in a shorter period of time on average and, even more important, their success rate is much higher than anywhere else in the world.[1]

Obviously, you can't expect the people involved with your investments to have the freedom to specialize and focus like the surgeons at Shouldice, but you do need to evaluate the experience of everyone involved in the investment—the overall company, the investment champions, the key decision makers, the team, the user base, and the shareholders—in terms of their experience with similar investments. The more experience on which you can draw, the more the investment's chances of success improve. There are sev-

---

1. For a more detailed discussion of the benefits of experience in medicine and, specifically, at Shouldice Hospital, see Atul Gawande, *Complications* (New York: Metropolitan Books, 2002).

eral things you should examine in the context of identifying and mitigating personnel experience risk:

- Compare the skills and knowledge of your team with the skills and knowledge needed to plan and execute the investment. If there are major gaps, you might need to bring in additional personnel, either from within or from outside of the company.

- The people in charge of executing an investment should have input into its design and planning to take advantage of their experience and insights, and to foster buy-in.

- Involve the investment's proponents in the execution of the investment, and involve team members in the planning stages of the investment. This reduces the risk of many potential problems, from communication breakdowns to misunderstanding goals, plans, and contingencies.

- Lack of familiarity or prior experience with your team or your vendor is an additional risk factor.

- It is dangerous to rely too much on a single individual, because there is no guarantee that individual will be around for the duration. Contingency plans to replace individuals and transfer knowledge among team members can reduce this risk factor considerably.

- Should the scope, schedule, or other factors and priorities in your company change suddenly, whether your team remains intact depends on the commitment of the company to your investment. Formal evaluations of availability and utilization efficiency can help ensure that you have the personnel resources that you need; these evaluations offer the additional benefit of reducing costs.

Buy-In and Corporate Culture: Getting buy-in from the major stakeholders is often overlooked in the evaluation and execution of investments, but it is absolutely critical to investment success. You need the consistent backing of investment champions and key decision makers to ensure that you will have the resources you need. Lack of commitment from your vendors or suppliers can have a similar effect. If end users resist, a perfectly executed investment from a technical perspective will still be a business failure. For investments that mostly affect employees, it's important to gain their support. Although this sounds obvious, many of us know from personal experience that some companies embark on investments, for example, in IT without taking the time or making sufficient efforts to get the people at the company to see the benefits and, accordingly, buy in. For investments that mostly affect customers, getting support means testing out concepts and prototypes with actual customers. Consider, for example, how Intuit has been able to develop products that are consistently easy to learn and easy to use. This success is not magic; it comes from an obsession at the company for making products that are easy to learn and easy to use. One of Intuit's ways of ensuring that its products are successful is by having labs where the company watches people use its software.

In both cases, this improves the chances that your investment will create value because people will actually use it. Other factors to consider include the following:

- The more stakeholders want your investment or believe they need it, the more cooperation and support you can expect to receive. This works both for key decision makers, who are much more likely to throw their support and resources behind an investment that they want or need, and for end users, who want their lives made simpler and will judge your investment accordingly. The less interest stakeholders have in your investment, the greater the risk it will fail.

- A formal approval process makes it much easier to determine the "end" of an investment. This reduces the risk of continuously changing demands and makes stakeholders more likely to be satisfied and cooperative.

- A final approval process sets clear criteria by which you can deem an investment finished. No matter how diligent you are in collecting requirements for an investment, stakeholders and end users will probably think of new requirements once they are exposed to your near-finished investment. Although occasionally these newfound "requirements" are indeed critical to the investment and require major changes, often they are not necessary for the investment to create value.

- Every investment needs a champion, a manager who has adopted the cause of the investment as his or her own and has the authority to ensure that sufficient personnel and resources are directed to it.

- Having specific procedures in place for resolving conflicts, making decisions, and communicating information can reduce the risk that your investment will run into difficulties from a conflict among stakeholders, a decision-making impasse, or the lack of some closely held and unshared key piece of information.

- A training program for end users can boost their understanding and acceptance of the investment; this helps reduce the risk that no one will use your investment, effectively making it a failure.

- No matter how well you define the requirements for a new investment, how long you labor over the execution plan, or how seamlessly you execute your plans, your investment might not work exactly as planned. Giving end users a mechanism with which to report problems and have questions answered can help improve the returns from your investment.

Research and Data Collection: Research and data collection are important components in the evaluation and execution of an investment. Using inaccurate data increases the risk that your analysis of an investment is wrong. Consider, for example, the assumptions that Disney made regarding guests length of stay at the hotels near Euro Disney. Drawing from its experiences at Disney World in Florida, the company made assumptions about how long visitors would stay at hotels near Euro Disney. Those estimates were factors in determining the number of hotel rooms the company built. Unfortunately, the company found in the early years of Euro Disney that its assumptions for the number of visitors overall to the park, and among those visitors the demand for hotel rooms, were too optimistic. (According to press reports, Euro Disney is now doing well.)

You can reduce the risk of ending up with wildly inaccurate cost and benefit estimates by carefully examining the underlying assumptions:

- Recognize the important assumptions and constraints that drive your cost and benefit analysis. Conduct a reality check on those values to see if they make common sense. For example, if the average COGS for your industry is 40 percent, you should be suspicious of an estimate that assumes 30 or even 35 percent COGS.

- Wherever possible, you should try and verify that your assumptions are appropriate for use with your particular investment. Although no amount of analysis can give you 100 percent confidence in your assumptions, you can significantly reduce your risk exposure through careful consideration of the assumptions you use.

Documentation: Your instinct might be to skimp on documentation and concentrate on just implementing your investment. After all, who likes paperwork and documentation plans? Fight this impulse, and make an effort to document fully the entire investment process. Proper documentation can be extremely helpful in eliminating many kinds of risk, and the information you record can also be helpful in future investments when you are seeking "lessons learned." Consider the following:

- Your plans require more than just detail. The risk-reducing effect of documentation depends on the quality of the execution plan and on your team's ability to follow the plan while retaining enough flexibility to adjust to any unexpected outcomes.

- A disciplined reporting process can help you spot problems early during the execution phase of your investment. Early detection often means the difference between a small, inexpensive adjustment at first or a major reengineering effort later on.

- By combining a formal, written process for instituting and tracking changes with an evaluation of the effect of changes on the overall investment, you can reduce the risk that changes will have an adverse impact on your investment.

Alignment and Benefits: To create value, your investment must be in line with the needs of your company, and it must deliver benefits that meet your company's needs when it is implemented. If not, you might be working at cross-purposes against the rest of the company; in the ensuing conflict, your investment is likely to fail. If your company is not able to use or incorporate the benefits your investment provides, that investment also is a failure. If your company doesn't need the benefits of your investment, you should not pursue it.

You should also be certain that the investment fits into, rather than works against, the corporate strategy of your company. This might seem like a small point, but it can have serious implications. For example, if your company is the acknowledged leader in premium quality for a product, your investment in an inexpensive line of similar goods could dilute the value of the brand. The earlier discussion regarding the Daimler-Benz acquisition of Chrysler is applicable here. Similarly, consider the reactions of some analysts to

Cisco's acquisition of Linksys. Several analysts have suggested that Linksys, a manufacturer of near-commodity-priced home networking gear with relatively low margins, was not a good acquisition for Cisco, a company used to developing and selling higher end networking equipment used by corporations. The acquisition, unlike most of the others made by Cisco in the past, simply did not appear to be in alignment with Cisco's business.

Think about what would happen to the value of your investment if the benefits it creates are fewer than expected. Your investment should be able to absorb at least some under performance, as investments should not be justified by razor-thin margins. Consider the percentage of the total functionality (benefits) you would need to receive from the investment for it to create value. Depending on the type of investment, you might not need to achieve all of the benefits for it to create value. This type of an investment is less risky than all-or-nothing investments. Thorough requirements gathering at the outset of the investment can limit benefits risk exposure.

Technology: Newer technologies generally carry greater risk than older, better established ones, because there is a greater chance that they won't work as expected. At the same time, older technology solutions usually do not offer the competitive advantages of more innovative solutions. If most of your competitors are already using a technology, the best you can hope for is to play catch-up, unless you take the risk and invest in newer, less proven technologies. You need to strike a balance between technological innovation and predictability.

Look at the specific circumstances that surround your choice of investment. Technology should not be an end unto itself, as evidenced by the failure of many investments made by businesses during the Internet bubble of the late 1990s. Technological investment alone is unlikely to create value; it must be combined with innovation in business processes to create sustainable value. You should try to focus on finding leading-edge technology investments that offer the greatest opportunity for creating competitive, sustainable differentiation. If your competitors are able to imitate your efforts quickly, the value you create by being the first to use a technology is minimal. In this case, you are probably better off waiting to invest until a technology becomes better established, less costly, and less risky. Let your competitors take on the risks of a cutting-edge technology, if you can catch up easily later on. You should invest in innovative technology, if, in doing so, you can create sustainable value.

The more established the technology, the lesser the potential for something to go wrong, but the smaller the opportunity to create significant value from the investment. You need to find a balance between pushing the technological envelope and minimizing the risk involved. Some investments, such as ERP software, might be well established but still require a great deal of customization to be useful to your company's unique business systems and processes. In this type of investment, the amount of customization required can have a great impact on risk; increased customization means resorting to less established procedures and structures, even if the underlying technology is well established.

Degree of Uncertainty

One way to categorize risk factors is by the degree of uncertainty inherent in them. As Donald Rumsfeld, Secretary of Defense, famously noted, there are "unknowns" and "unknown unknowns" when you consider risks. Although all risks represent uncertainty, some are clearly more uncertain than others. In a software investment, you should plan for the possibility that software bugs could delay the investment. This might or might not happen, but it is a distinct enough possibility that you should be prepared for it. On the other hand, unless your facility is near a fault line, you should probably not spend long hours planning for an earthquake. To formalize this process, use the following five categories: noise, minor events, known unknowns, unknown unknowns, and messes. Depending on the particulars of the investment itself, the risk factors involved in an investment will be a combination of some or all of these categories. Let's take a closer look at each category.

Noise: Inevitably, you will discover a range of issues that at first appear to warrant concern and planning, but are not significant to the overall success of your investment. Make sure that you take the time to differentiate what is actionable and what should be ignored. Be careful, however, to make sure that what you think is "noise" is, indeed, noise from the perspective of your stakeholders. For example, several years ago, the domestic manufacturers of cars, the so-called Big Three of General Motors, Ford, and Chrysler, thought that minor variations in the "fit and finish" of cars simply were not important enough to justify the time and effort required to build systems to eliminate these variations. The quality levels of their cars were "good enough." These companies found, however, that minor variations in fit and finish were not noise to many consumers once they saw and experienced cars made abroad that had superior quality.

Minor Events: Minor events can be caused by many subtle factors and influences that together can cause a range of effects on an investment, but are difficult to measure individually. It is seldom worth your while to attempt to track down the specific causes of minor events. To see how minor events can affect an investment, think about an investment that spans several months and involves the work of several different people. You would break this investment up into hundreds of small tasks that are scheduled to take one person one hour, for example. It is easy to imagine with the investment broken up into such small, discrete pieces, that a specific task could get delayed by unexpected meetings, a doctor's appointment, or just slightly misjudging the time it takes to complete the task.

The effect of a delay on one task is tiny in the context of the overall investment, and you would not want to devote any time to planning specifically for something this insignificant. If you multiply these same effects over the hundreds of tasks included in an investment, the overall effect is much more noticeable. If every task takes an hour longer than scheduled, and there are 100 tasks, the overall effect is 100 hours! In an investment dominated by minor events, the objectives and the sequences and details of the activities are well defined and stable, but a number of factors can cause the budgets and schedules to shift. To deal with these minor events, therefore, focus on the cumulative impact from changes in budgets and schedules that result from the minor events, rather than on the events themselves. Think of a snowball rolling downhill, picking up additional incremental amounts of snow, and constantly gaining momentum as it goes along. If snow conditions are right, and the hill is long enough, the snowball will have tremendous size and impact when it reaches the bottom.

Known Unknowns: Known unknowns are risk factors with effects that are distinct, identifiable, and likely enough that you should have a contingency plan if they do occur. Unlike minor events, where contingency plans should focus on the combined results of events, your contingency plans should deal directly with known unknown risk factors. For example, in software investments, the amount of customization required to get a software system to meet its particular needs is a critical driver of cost and schedule. The exact amount of customization required is often difficult or impossible to determine beforehand because users inevitably learn more about what they want and need as part of the execution process. Think about when you are decorating a new room or moving furniture. The process involves constant changes and, often, a recognition that you need to go out and get another piece of furniture or decorative item. Careful requirements gathering and planning will go a long way toward defining the amount of customization needed, but even with careful planning, there is still a distinct possibility that additional unplanned customization work might still be required.

Unknown Unknowns (Unforeseen Certainty) : Like a known unknown, unknown unknowns have identifiable and distinct effects. However, the difference between them is that unknown unknowns cannot be identified or predicted during the planning phase of an investment, either because you are unaware of them, or you consider them too unlikely to worry about. Unknown unknowns can result from totally unexpected events or they might arise from the interaction of many different events that were individually foreseen, but the interactions of which caused unexpected results. Investments focused on new technologies or new markets are particularly susceptible to unknown unknowns, which is not surprising, because both types of investments are in uncharted territory. For example, the development of Ivory soap by Proctor & Gamble was accidental. Reportedly, the person responsible for watching the vat accidentally discovered a soap product that could float. Unlike the result of many unknown unknowns, Ivory soap was a positive outcome, but it was an unexpected event.

There are two keys to managing unknown unknowns. The first is to recognize them as early as possible. Second, you need to combine flexibility in addressing problems with an established change management methodology to deal with them quickly and efficiently as soon as they arise.

Messes: Messes happen when objectives, assumptions, and execution plans are unstable, unpredictable, or fluid throughout the duration of the investment. Messes dominate investments when technology is in complete upheaval or when R&D is focused on research rather than development. Research investments typically have a defined goal, but there is no specific end product in mind. This type of investment is typical in the pharmaceutical industry, where new products often emerge from basic scientific research. Consider, for example, Merck's experience with the drug Aprepitant, which the company hoped would be a major player in the antidepressant market. After spending more than 10 years and untold millions of dollars, the company recently decided to end research on the drug as a treatment for depression. Yet, in the late 1990s the company considered the drug to have tremendous potential.

The key to managing risks in investments, characterized by messes, is to maintain flexibility and focus on iteration (incremental improvements) as the major underlying investment management structure.

Table 5.1 shows the major differences among noise, minor events, known unknown, unknown unknowns, and mess risk factors. Dealing with these risk factors requires different types of planning, infrastructure, and chaos. Managing minor events requires monitoring and planning for the changes in budget and schedule that result from those events, but not the events themselves. Known unknown risk factors are predictable and distinguishable enough that they might merit their own contingency plans in preparation for the possible occurrence of each risk. Unknown unknowns are not predictable, so you cannot plan for specific risk factors.

Table 5.1 Characteristics of Risk Factors by Degree of Uncertainty

Uncertainty Category	Distinct Effect?	Identifiable Effect?	Predictable?	Objectives Stable?	Plan Stable?	Risk Management Techniques
Noise	No	No	No	Yes	Yes	Ignore
Minor Events	No	No	Yes	Yes	Yes	Contingency plans for budget and schedule effects of variation
Known Unknown	Yes	Yes	Yes	Yes	Yes	Contingency plans for known/unknown risk factors
Unknown Unknown	Yes	Yes	No	Yes	Yes	Monitoring change management plans
Chaos	Yes	Yes	No	Yes	No	Flexibility, iteration

Instead, you should focus on putting systematic change management procedures in place to minimize the damage to your investment when they do occur. Finally, mess risk factors require an iterative, flexible approach to investments that minimize and delay commitment to a particular path while allowing the uncertainties to play themselves out.

Probability

To repeat a point from the beginning of the chapter, it makes common sense to prepare for the things that are the most likely to occur. If the weather report calls for a 90 percent chance of rain, you probably should carry an umbrella. If the chance of rain is negligible, carrying an umbrella around is probably a waste of effort, and you might feel silly doing it. You can apply this same common sense approach to business investments—it is usually a waste of resources to plan for remote possibilities.

How do you determine whether a risk is likely enough that you should include it in your contingency plans? There are a number of different ways to measure probability, depending on the time and information available to you. Possible measurement scales include the following:

- *Probability:* Quantify the chance of each risk happening using a number between 0 and 1 or 0 percent and 100 percent (0 means it will never occur, and 100 means the event will always occur).

- *Low–Medium–High:* Assign risks to one of three categories of occurrence: low probability, medium probability, or high probability of occurrence.

- *Rank in order of likelihood of occurrence:* Put your risks in order, from most likely to occur to least likely to occur, without assigning numeric probabilities to each risk.

As you can see, these scales vary considerably in their precision. Remember, it does you no good to estimate risk probabilities precisely if you cannot estimate them accurately. In many cases, it might not be worth the time and effort to assign precise probabilities. Even if you did, your estimates would still depend on untested assumptions. The primary purpose of using this technique is to find and limit the major sources of risk to an investment, not to develop a minutely detailed reckoning of risk priorities.

How do you assign probabilities or probability categories to risks in the first place? The answer depends on the nature of the investment you are considering, the amount of information you have available, and your experience with similar investments. If you have enough experience, you can look at how many times each risk actually has occurred in the past in your lessons learned files or records, but you would need a sufficiently robust set of lessons learned files or records of previous investments. You would also need to use prior investments that are as similar as possible to the one you are currently considering. The larger the number of investments and the more similar they are to the current investment, the better your estimates are likely to be.

For many investments, this approach is simply not possible or practical. If this is a new type of investment for you or your company, you will need to make estimates based in part on your prior experiences and your associates', even if they are not exactly the same as the investment you are considering. One way is to ask a number of experienced people how they rate various risks and look at the aggregate results using a formal survey methodology. Ask respondents to answer individually and then discuss in a group. The potential pitfalls of arriving at a group consensus can, therefore be avoided, and it uses standard rating scales so that responses can be properly compared. If the most knowledgeable people believe a risk is highly likely to occur, you probably should pay close attention to it. The point is to hone in on the important risks, not to pin down the exact probability that a given event will occur.

Impact of Risks

Fundamentally, there are only three possible ways risks can impact your investment; risks can have an impact on the following:

1. *Functionality:* The investment does not provide the expected features, functionalities, or benefits.

2. *Schedule:* The investment takes longer than expected to implement.

3. *Cost:* The investment costs more than expected.

These three effects are themselves interrelated because they all boil down to a single, crucial figure, the value of your investment. If an investment falls behind schedule, it is either going to cost more in time and resources to get caught up, or the scope of the investment will have to be cut to make the deadline. As we will see in the next chapter, scope (functionality), schedule, and budget (cost) are key metrics. Because some risk factors could have an impact in two or even all three areas, you should evaluate the potential impact of each risk factor for its effect on functionality, schedule, and cost. In effect, you need to create a series of scenarios that enable the development of contingency plans that adjust time, scope, and budget.

Creating a Risk Profile

Now that you have an idea of the source, the degree of uncertainty, the probability, and the potential impact on functionality, schedule and budget, you can use this information to develop a risk profile for your investment. The examination of risk sources helped you to identify the risk factors your investment faces, and the level of uncertainty is most usefully applied to the risks of your investment in the aggregate, to see what types of risk dominate in your investment. You can then look at each of the risks you have identified in terms of their probability and their impact on budget, schedule, and functionality, in conjunction with each other. Using this analysis, any risk factor that ranks as high–high (as in high probability, high impact) should be of special concern.

A useful way to get a sense of the overall risk of your investment is to plot the probability and impact of each risk factor in a

3-by-3 matrix of high, medium, and low probability and high, medium, and low impact, as shown in Figure 5.2. You can either do this separately for functionality, schedule, and budget, or you can plot all three on top of each other. You can get an idea of the overall risk profile of your investment depending on where your risk factors map to the grid. If most of the risk factors cluster in the top right quadrant, you have a lot of potential problems to worry about, because they have a high probability of occurrence and will have a major impact if they do occur. On the other hand, if they cluster to the lower left quadrant, your investment appears to be relatively low risk. These risk factors are unlikely to occur, and, if they do, they will not have a major impact.

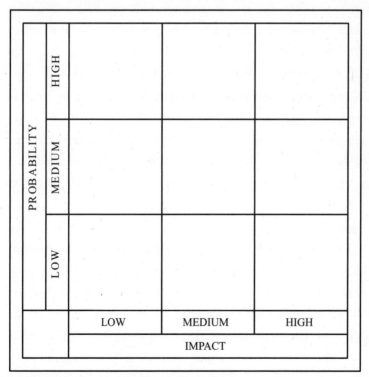

Figure 5.2   3 × 3 Probability/Impact Matrix

Pulling Risk and Return Together

Once you have a good sense of the magnitude of risks and the impacts, you can map those risks relative to returns as shown in Figure 5.3. The return (ROI) and the risk of an investment are mapped together.

Incremental Revenue: The top left quadrant, with a high ROI and low risk, is called incremental revenue and encompasses investments such as product or service line extensions. Think of the impact on revenues, profits, and cash flow of a new product or service that is very similar to what your company already offers. The investment required for a product or service line extension is much less than that for a completely new product or service because your company already has experience making and selling similar offerings, a likely customer base is already in place, and the "retooling" necessary to produce the new offering is minimal.

In this case, the relatively high ROI is driven more by the low investment costs for the incremental revenue than by a major increase in revenues. The risks involved in line extension are much less than for a new line of products or services because your company already knows what is required to execute such an investment successfully.

Consider Nabisco's experience with Oreo cookies. A few years ago, Nabisco began to introduce Oreo cookies in different sizes and flavors. The investment in these product line extensions was not significant compared to an investment in an unrelated new product. Nabisco faced relatively little risk with these variations on Oreos. The Oreo brand was successful, and the company knew its customers. The success of the new products (Oreos with orange filling at Halloween, Oreos with red filling in December, fudge-covered or white chocolate-dipped Oreos for the holidays, and Oreos with blue

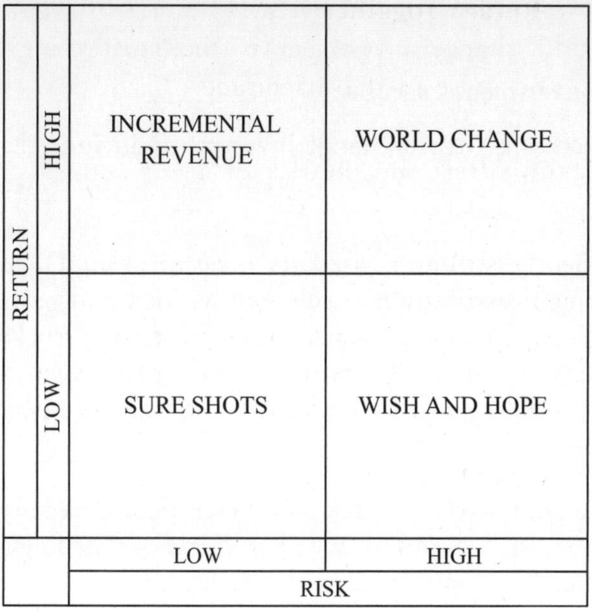

Figure 5.3 The Risk/Return Matrix

filling in the spring for Easter) has brought incremental revenue and profits to Nabisco. In this case, execution required that Nabisco make minor modifications to its strategy with Oreo, and management had nearly complete control over this execution process.

World Change: Investments in the top right quadrant have high risks and high potential returns, and are called world change investments. This category includes investments such as major acquisitions, new products, or investments in major software systems like ERP or CRM. A successful world change investment will have a major impact on revenue, profits, and cash flows. It can potentially transform a business. There are major risks associated with these investments, particularly because so many factors are not directly within management's control. Control over execution is limited; even if management does its best work, the investment can still fail. How successfully you can navigate the risks involved in executing a world change investment is the most critical determinant of the investment's success.

Examples of successful world change investments include the following:

- Cemex, a cement distributor, used its investment in IT to change the cement distribution business in Mexico and parts of the United States by more efficient use of its delivery trucks and better service to time-sensitive contractors. Cemex changed the ground rules in its industry through its savvy implementation of IT systems.

- Eli Lilly was a middle-of-the-pack pharmaceutical company until it made a major bet on Prozac. The success of that single drug helped make the company an industry leader.

Sure Shots: Investments with low returns and low risks, in the bottom left quadrant, are called sure shot investments. They typically focus on reducing the costs of doing business, and they are sometimes referred to as optimization. Sure shot investments dominate corporate capital spending today, as companies focus almost exclusively on ways to reduce expenses.

For sure shot investments, the execution process is relatively easy because it generally follows a proven strategy. Additionally, management knows that once the investment is up and running, it is nearly certain to provide cost savings. The benefits with sure shots generally fall below the revenue line on the income statement. Management controls expenses and knows that if it can reduce expenses there will be a positive impact on the bottom line. Relative to incremental revenue investment opportunities, the return on sure shot investments is usually lower, and the execution focus is on expense and cost reduction as opposed to revenue growth.

Two recent examples of successful sure shot investments are as follows:

- Mercedes-Benz USA recently invested in an e-learning system. The company decided to make the investment based on two factors: First, the ROI was positive, and, second, once operational, the system would provide significant savings in travel costs and lost time for personnel away from the office. The investment has proven to be very successful in reducing costs, but it has not had a direct impact on revenue.

- Amtrak invested in a voice recognition system that substitutes for live operators in assisting customers with schedules and fares. This investment has resulted in tremendous cost savings in personnel time, but it has not increased revenue.

You should be concerned with two major issues when considering sure shot investments. From an internal perspective, you should ask yourself and the members of your team, "What risks and risk mitigation strategies should we adopt to improve the odds that we will execute the investment successfully?" You should also ask "Who benefits from the returns?"

You have many investment opportunities with the potential of increasing your bottom-line profits by reducing your costs and expenses. If your competition, however, undertakes the same types of investments, it will lead to a lower cost structure across the industry, as discussed earlier. Many of us have experienced this with an ATM at virtually of our neighborhood banks. In effect, you and your competitors will have pounded each other with two by fours; the end result is that some companies are forced to leave the industry, and the survivors have lower overall profitability and returns to their shareholders.

You can usually analyze and justify sure shot investments with classical finance tools such as ROI. The costs of the investment are easy to identify, as are the returns from the investment.

Management needs only to execute them internally to achieve the promised results.

Wish and Hope: The bottom right quadrant is for investments with low returns and high risk, called wish and hope investments. Wish and hope investments represent the worst of both worlds: Execution cannot effectively mitigate the risks for relatively low returns. Many of the "if you build it they will come" investments in e-commerce and telecommunications discussed in an earlier chapter fall within this category. Some managers make these investments, even when the evidence of failure is obvious. The common maxim, "sometimes the easiest person to fool is yourself" comes to mind.

Consider, for example, the investments made by telecoms in infrastructure to carry Internet traffic. During the late 1990s, well over $500 billion was spent building capacity to handle the seemingly unlimited growth in Internet traffic. Many of these telecommunications investments were made, believe it or not, primarily on the single presumption that Internet traffic was growing at a rate of over 100 percent per month. Given the fact that executives were betting hundreds of millions of dollars of their shareholders' money, you would think that they would investigate and confirm this assumed growth number. As strange as it might sound today, the so-called experts making these investment decisions did less research than many of us do when buying furniture, cars, or durable goods. More specifically, they didn't confirm the validity of the 100 percent per month growth assumption. In fact, anyone who would have taken the time to investigate the projected Internet growth would have quickly learned that it was wrong. Wishing and hoping ruled the day.

Just as surprisingly, the telecommunications infrastructure investments were made without much thought about how the growth would be achieved. Even if we give them the benefit of the doubt that the projected 100 percent per month growth in Internet traffic was a reasonable assumption, few executives put much thought into how their companies would be able to capture this growth profitably beyond just laying cable and waiting for customers. Many people talked about the "last mile" of copper wire between households and the fiber, but there is still no economically viable solution for getting to household end users except by linking to them directly. Growth in this sector has been much slower than anticipated, and as of mid-2003, less than 15 percent of the fiber installed was in use.

Wish and hope investments are not limited to technology. For example, think about Quality Dining's acquisition of Bruegger's Bagels. Less than one year after paying about $100 million for Bruegger's Bagels, Quality's management realized that the retail bagel business had minimal barriers to entry. It also found that running bagel shops was more difficult and obviously less profitable then they thought, and the company sold Bruegger's back to many of the original owners at a substantial loss.

What to Do With the Risk–Return Matrix

You can use the risk–return matrix in several ways. You can use it as a stepping-off point in looking for investments for your company that fit into the results that you want to achieve. If you want incremental revenue, but inadvertently pursue a world change investment, you are likely to be in for an unpleasant surprise. You should also use the matrix as a screening tool to weed out unwise or inappropriate investments. Under no circumstances should you pursue an investment that offers low returns in exchange for high risk. You might not be able to identify an investment as such unless you study it carefully. Finally, knowing where your investment is located on this matrix can help put you in the proper mindset to address the risks you are likely to face.

Risk Mitigation Plans

Once you have a clear idea of the risks you need to worry about and plan for, you can develop mitigation plans to minimize any adverse effects on your investment. Thus, mitigation plans will increase the likelihood of success for your investment. There are a number of ways you can address a given risk factor (some clearly better than others), so many that we will not go into a long laundry list of different plans here. An important component of risk mitigation is ongoing management, the topic of a later chapter. As part of ongoing management, you'll need to reassess risks constantly and take actions when needed.

There are certain procedures, such as measuring and monitoring methodologies, that you can apply to nearly any investment to reduce risk markedly. Other mitigation plans will be specific to your investment and the risk factor you are trying to address. The key is to be prepared. For example, in your car trip from Los Angeles to Boston, one risk mitigation plan is to make sure that the car has a spare tire. If, however, you plan to fly to Boston, the tire in the trunk of your car doesn't mitigate any risk.

You should evaluate closely a complicated or expensive risk mitigation plan like any other investment. Each plan has its own risks and rewards. The cost of mitigation needs to be weighted against the impact on your investment should the risks occur. You cannot consider risk mitigation plans either in a vacuum or as a way to reduce risk for its own sake. Your sole objective in reducing risk is to improve the chances that your investment will be successful; as a result, you need to evaluate a risk mitigation plan in the context of your entire investment plan. Consider the effects it will have on cost, scheduling, and functionality to make sure that your efforts are adding, rather than subtracting, value from your investment.

Summary

This chapter gave you a framework for identifying risk factors by their source, degree of uncertainty, probability, and impact. Not all of these factors will apply to each investment that you consider, but you should take the time to review potential risk factors for every investment proposal. From the information you collect, you can develop a risk profile to help you identify the most significant risks, those risks that are the most likely to occur, and those that will have the greatest impact on schedule, budget, or functionality. These risks should be the focus of your risk mitigation plans, as you do not have the time or the resources to worry about every risk.

The risk profile also enables you to map the risks of your investment against the potential returns to classify it as an incremental revenue, world change, sure shot, or wish and hope investment. Each of these categories requires different risk management and investment management techniques. Wish and hope investments, which provide low returns at a high risk, should generally be avoided. Finally, it is critical that you develop risk mitigation plans for the most important risks your investment faces. These mitigation plans should add value to, rather than drain value from your investment by improving the likelihood of success that will grow corporate value.

Following the Roadmap

Fresh Breeze is considering investing in an ERP software system that would integrate the company's distribution, procurement, and financial systems. These functions are currently handled by several legacy software systems. The company has vetted the investment proposal through a preliminary analysis, where it was found to provide substantial benefits. The business impact analysis showed that the investment would be consistent with the company's value drivers.

The next step is to perform a comprehensive risk analysis on the investment. Using the Business Investment Roadmap, the external macro and other risks were identified. Although some risk factors were discovered in the external macro portion of the analysis, these were not major contributors to the risk of the overall investment. More specifically, Fresh Breeze's risk analysis found the following significant risk factors:

- *Duration and timing:* Due to the nature of ERP software and Fresh Breeze's size and organizational complexity, this investment will be a major undertaking. In all likelihood, it will take months to plan and to implement the system across all of its business units.

- *Personnel experience, availability, and buying:* Beyond the investment's champion, Fresh Breeze has few personnel resources experienced in large-scale software implementations; thus, it must rely to a large extent on outside resources to implement the system.

- *Research and data collection:* Fresh Breeze must clearly identify and perform checks on the assumptions and constraints that will drive the value of its software investment. This vetting process ultimately involves incorporating risk and risk management into the cost–benefit analysis for the investment.

- *Planning:* Fresh Breeze must build a schedule and budget from the ground up, starting from the required features and functions, and then establishing the time and resources required to meet each of those objectives.

- *Documentation and performance measurement:* Fresh Breeze must closely and carefully document all aspects of an investment of this complexity, including detailed requirements, execution plans, budget, and user and training documentation. It also needs to develop performance targets and measures, which it can use to gauge performance quickly, and make decisions on how and whether to continue throughout the duration of the investment.

- *Alignment and benefits:* Fresh Breeze's needs are well defined for this investment, and it is in line with overall company strategy. The company estimates that it would still create value with this investment if the system achieves only 70 percent of the expected functionality. The detailed requirements of the system remain a major concern and risk factor, but this risk will hopefully be mitigated as the requirements are collected and analyzed.

Of the factors just considered, personnel experience and implementation have the greatest probability of affecting the investment, although planning and operating risk factors also are likely to affect the investment. Finally, the company must consider how different risk factors have different effects on budget, schedule, and functionality if they occur. For example, if timing and duration issues, occur, thye are likely to have a major impact on the budget and schedule but not much of an impact on the functionality or scope. Unless schedule and budget problems are so tremendous that scope cuts need to be made, delays are unlikely to affect the functionality of the software. On the other hand, if the investment experiences documentation-related issues, the impact on functionality is likely to be very high, whereas the effect on schedule and budget will be much less significant. Some risk factors, such as implementation, could have a serious impact on budget, schedule, and functionality.

Figure 5.4 maps the probability and impact data from Fresh Breeze into the 3 × 3 probability and impact matrix discussed earlier. As you can see, budget and schedule are more likely to be strongly impacted by risk than schedule, because more of the risk factors cluster on the right and upper right side of the matrix for budget and schedule. Taken together, the investment has medium to medium-high overall risk.

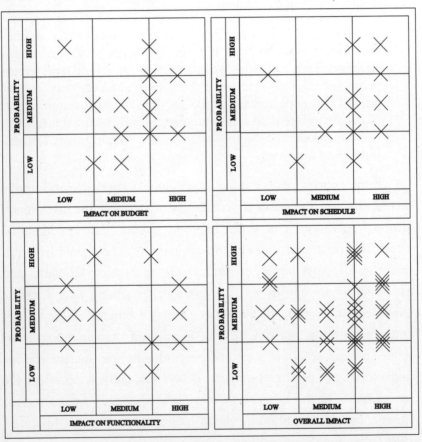

Figure 5.4   Fresh Breeze Software Implementation 3 × 3 Risk Factor Probability Versus Impact on Cost, Schedule, Functionality, and Overall Impact

From this analysis, Fresh Breeze will be able to determine the important risks it faces with this investment, and it will be able to include contingency plans for these risks. In comparing the risks of the investment with potential returns, Fresh Breeze finds that the ERP is likely to be a world change investment, because it is likely to transform the company. Also, an investment of such complexity has high risks. This analysis allows the company to develop mitigation plans. Some particularly important features of this mitigation plan include the following:

- Choosing a reliable and easily customizable ERP system and a competent systems integrator.

- Employing standard project management methodologies throughout the process, including tracking progress.

6

EXECUTION ANALYSIS

Execution is the great unaddressed issue in the business world today. Its absence is the single biggest obstacle to success and the cause of most of the disappointments that are mistakenly attributed to other causes.

Larry Bossidy and Ram Charan in
Execution: The Discipline of Getting Things Done

The importance of execution to creating corporate value through investments is a primary focus in this book. Execution is what bridges the gap between strategies and financial metrics. An investment can pass the strategy review and financial analysis, but, it will fail by definition if it is not executed well. Howard Geneen, the leader of what was once one of the world's largest conglomerates, ITT, noted, "I think it is an immutable law in business that words are words, explanations are explanations, promises are promises—but only performance is reality." Execution is performance.

Execution analysis involves developing a fundamental under-standing of the who, what, when, where, why, and how of your investment, and the impact your investment will have on your customers. The answers to these questions will provide you with the details that you must use to evaluate your investment thoroughly and minimize the risk of failure. There is nothing special or unique about these questions, but if you cover these details before your company makes a decision to invest, you won't have to scramble when problems occur later on.

This process is analogous to creating and evaluating the working drawings for a construction project. The working drawings, and the details underlying them, allow a contractor to estimate the cost and the time needed to build a structure. With the "working drawings" of your investment in hand, you can more accurately forecast the resources you need and the trade-offs that might be necessary to make your investment a success. It is always easier to make those trade-offs early in the process, before you have lost significant time and money and an internal bias and constituency for the investment. Just as importantly, with a detailed execution plan in place, you can more easily assess the impact of changes due to market conditions, internal corporate issues, or other factors. By doing so, you will be able to develop alternatives that enable the investment to be successful, and ultimately grow corporate value.

Your execution analysis also must consider the availability of resources, especially capital, needed to ensure the success of your investment. In addition, it is critical that you determine the impact your investment will have on your customers and prospects, because customers are the lifeblood of any business.

Fortunately, you already have begun the execution analysis element of the Business Investment Roadmap as part of the preliminary analysis. In the preliminary analysis that you began to consider ways that your company can grow revenue and reduce costs. You also considered capital intensity and the impact on your customers. Now, your analysis goes into more depth; you are really peeling deeply into that onion that had only the first-level cuts in the preliminary analysis.

This chapter explains how to:

1. Determine the who, what, when, where, why, and how needed to execute your investment successfully.

2. Determine the capital intensity of your investment.

3. Determine the impact of the investment on customers and prospects.

Each of these issues is critical to making a investment that grows corporate value. As shown in Figure 6.1, execution analysis is the fourth element of the Business Investment Roadmap.

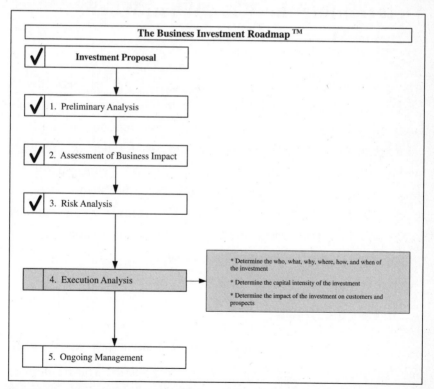

Figure 6.1   Decision Route: The Business Investment Roadmap: Execution Analysis

REVIEW	Review the who, what, where, why, when, and how of the investment with it's major proponents critically and in detail.
TIMING AND SEQUENCE	Investigate the timing and sequence of the investment in terms of the required order of events and competing priorities at your company.
TRADEOFFS	Consider the tradeoffs you will need to make between schedule, budget, and scope.
HOW MANY YESES	Determine how many people need to be involved or to give approval for the investment to succeed.

Figure 6.2   Four Steps to Confronting the Details of Your Investment

Determining the Who, What, When, Where, Why, and How

The old saying, "the devil is in the details" applies perfectly to business investments. Pay insufficient attention to the details of your investment and, you put it at a heightened risk of failure. Embark on an investment without answering the who, what, when, where, why, and how, you might get lucky and avoid major problems, but you are much more likely to be sidelined by unforeseen problems. If you do not work through these critical questions, trouble will eventually catch up with you. How do you confront the details of your investment? Figure 6.2 outlines an approach.

Review the Details

Review the who, what, when, where, why, and how of an investment with its major backers and proponents. You need more than a laundry list here; draw up a complete map of the investment that tracks it from start to finish. Be as detailed as possible. For example, determine the amount of effort and what each individual involved needs to devote to the investment, and list in detail and confirm the availability of all of the resources you need.

Do not cut slack to your investment's proponents in this phase of your execution analysis, especially if you are its major champion. Missing information and guesstimates based on little more than hope are likely to result in major problems. When in doubt, drill down further for more detail. For example, many software companies have found that the best way to ensure the success of their investments in the development of new products is to track the daily work efforts of their programmers.

Timing and Sequence

If you are baking a cake, you can't put the cake in the oven before you mix the ingredients together. Although the mixing order does not matter for some recipes, you wouldn't add frosting to the cake batter before putting it in the oven or bake the cake and then mix it. Your cake will be a disaster if you don't mix the ingredients together at all, or if you do not combine them in the proper sequence, even if you use the exact amount of each ingredient specified.

Timing and sequence is just as important in your business investments. Consider investments by retailers in software to maximize the profitability of in-store promotions. This type of software has been proven to be effective in raising margins at chains like Long's Drugs, a major retailer in the western United States. Even with the promise of high ROIs and the proof of success, many retailers have not yet invested in this software, in large part because of a more pressing need to invest first in more essential systems for distribution and logistics.

Trade-Offs

At a basic level, the success of your investment depends on how well you manage your resources, time, and scope. Changes in any of these three critical inputs necessitate changes in the others. The relationship of resources, time, and scope is often referred to by project managers and engineers as the *iron triangle* because the three factors cannot be changed independently (see Figure 6.3).

It is often difficult to accept the iron triangle's immutable relationships. It would be great if you could cut resources without a negative impact on time and scope. With rare exceptions, this is impossible; if you cut resources, you must either reduce scope or expand time. There are no other alternatives. Keep the iron triangle in mind as you review the working drawings of your investment. If your investment requires more financial and per-

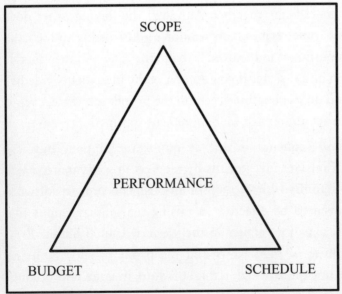

Figure 6.3   The Iron Triangle of Investment Scope, Budget, and Schedule

sonnel resources than you originally thought, accept a time delay or a reduction in scope *sooner* rather than later. Consider, for example, the Big Dig, Boston's massive construction project and the nation's largest public works investment. The Big Dig is substantially over budget and behind schedule, not an unusual situation for a public works project. One of the causes of the delays and cost overruns, however, was a decision to cut corners regarding one component of the project, a tunnel from the Massachusetts Turnpike. The tunnel ended up with major leaks, and the problem required a significant investment in time and resources to remedy.

How Many Yeses

You can use a reality check for your answers to who, what, when, where, why, and how, called "How many yeses?" Always ask the investment's proponents, "How many people must be involved along the way, and how many of those people must approve (say 'yes') to make the investment successful?" To illustrate the importance of asking how many yeses, consider Keurig, a company with a patent on a coffee dispenser and brewing system that eliminates the need for packaged coffee and traditional office brewing methods.

The Keurig system is simple, easy to use, and eliminates messy cleanups and moldy coffee pots. It also allows you to brew individual servings of coffee rather than a whole pot, which has obvious benefits in the office kitchen. Who wants coffee out of a pot that looks like a science experiment?

Keurig has not achieved the success that its founders and financial backers anticipated. There are several reasons why Keurig has not met expectations, but one of them is the six levels of approval it needs to secure to get end users for its system. Working backwards, these are:

1. The coffee drinker who decides to use the Keurig system in his or her office.

2. The office manager who decides to have the machine installed.

3. The coffee distributor salesperson who decides to promote Keurig to his or her customers (the office managers).

4. The coffee distributor who decides to carry the Keurig brewers and creates incentives for the sales force to promote Keurig.

5. The manufacturer that decides to make the brewing systems.

6. The coffee company that agrees to package its products in the Keurig patented dispensers.

Keurig faces the difficult challenge of getting six different levels of yes to deliver its products to end users, which has dampened the company's success. In the face of these challenges, the company has recently sought to sell its brewing systems directly to consumers, thus reducing the number of yeses needed to achieve success.

Determining Capital Intensity

The second step in execution analysis examines the capital intensity of investments. An ideal investment would increase sales without requiring any investments in additional fixed or working capital (i.e., the proverbial mailbox that collects checks from customers). In the real world, nearly all increases in sales require investments in fixed capital, working capital (inventory, accounts receivable), additional personnel, and other sales-related expenses. You must subtract these increases in working capital and cash investments in fixed assets from accounting profits to calculate cash flows. The cash flow benefit of an investment decreases with increases in fixed and working capital. In comparing two investments with the same expected increase in sales, the investment with lower capital requirements is usually a better opportunity. Similarly, investments that promote greater increases in sales for a given level of capital requirements are usually better.

How should you think about execution in the context of capital intensity? The answer is twofold; you must measure the capital intensity, and you must confirm that your company is willing and able to commit the capital necessary for the investment itself as well as on an ongoing basis. For example, the development of a new product line typically requires a major capital investment, but you also must continue to provide the product line with additional capital until it becomes cash-flow positive. Think of the General Motors investment in Saturn discussed in an earlier chapter.

Determining the capital intensity is actually pretty simple: add fixed assets and net working capital together, and divide the result by sales. The resulting figure, the capital intensity ratio, describes the capital investment needed to generate a dollar of sales. Although you can apply this ratio to your company's sales and assets as a whole, it is often more useful to consider the capital intensity of your investment separately, using the ratio of the incremental capital increases and incremental sales increases. Investments with high capital intensities create less value in the form of free cash flows. They are riskier because they require a larger asset investment. Capital-intense investments are not inherently bad; often they are necessary or even desirable given the nature of an industry. You should use this ratio as a way to compare investment options and in your overall evaluation of an investment.

The second element of the capital intensity evaluation is a bit more difficult. You must consider the length and the scope of the capital commitment required to finish and maintain your investment on an ongoing basis. As part of these projections, you must anticipate surprises that will inevitably arise and require you to invest more capital. Is your company prepared to continue the investment, or will the continual need for capital force you to ask whether you are throwing away good money after bad?

The Impact of an Investment on Customers

The final step of execution analysis involves understanding how an investment is likely to affect your customers. Customers are at the root of virtually everything your company does; they are your reason for existing as an enterprise. You have already seen how to evaluate a potential investment by its impact on revenues and costs. Customers are the source of your revenue, and revenue projections depend entirely on new and continued sales to these customers. Customers are probably the most important assets your company has!

Your customer base does not show up directly on your balance sheet, in spite of its importance of an asset, but many transactions are based on acquiring customers. Making an informed decision on an acquisition method requires you to know the value of those customers. You must also consider the impact of any investment on your existing customers, whether the aim of the investment is to increase sales or to decrease costs.

Linking Investments to Your Customers

As discussed earlier in the chapters on preliminary analysis and bang for the buck, companies make two types of investments:

revenue growth investments (the top of the income statement) or cost reduction and productivity investments (the bottom of the income statement). You must consider the impact of both types of investments on your customers because any effect on your customers ultimately impacts your revenues and profits.

Cost Reduction and Productivity Investments

The goal of a cost reduction or productivity investment is to reduce your direct or indirect expenses, by producing the same amount of goods or services at a lower cost. Many investments designed to lower operating costs do not have an immediately obvious, direct effect on customers. It is still important, however, to look at the investment in the context of how it changes the customer experience. You should examine in detail all of the points at which the customer will have contact with the new investment, either directly, as in an automated phone directory, or indirectly, as in whether your employees will be equipped and willing to help customers who call. The cost savings you assumed in your analysis ultimately depend on maintaining or increasing your sales. If you lose more customers than you expected, the bottom line cost savings benefits you assumed might evaporate.

Consider a shoe manufacturer that invests in a new device that enables it to manufacture the same number of shoes at a lower cost. The company becomes more productive, and its profits increase compared to its profitability prior to the investment. However, if the new production process negatively impacts the quality of the shoes, the company will lose customers. The cost reduction investment, therefore, will not work, because success is predicated on sustaining sales levels.

Companies tend to emphasize cost reduction investments during uncertain or difficult economic environments, and often they do have an immediate impact on the bottom line. Cost reduction investments can lead a company to a business model that is superior to those of its competitors. Southwest Airlines, for example, has a much lower seat cost per mile (a common metric used by airline companies) than most other airlines. One of the ways that Southwest Airlines has lowered its costs relative to its competitors is that it has only one type of plane in its fleet, the Boeing 737. The cost savings are significant, both in the reduced training for pilots and staff and in lower maintenance costs. Pilots and staff must learn only one type of aircraft. Southwest needs to stock spare parts for only one type of airplane type versus many types of planes.

Revenue Growth Investments

The objective of a revenue growth investment is to increase the top line of the income statement (sales). In terms of products you sell and the customers you sell them to, there are four ways to increase revenues, as illustrated in Figure 6.4, commonly called the Ansoff matrix. Increasing revenues might involve selling more existing products to existing customers, selling existing products to new customers, selling new products to existing customers, or selling new products to new customers.

Sell Existing Products to Existing Customers (Market Penetration): By selling more of your existing products and services to existing customers, you grow the value of the customer relationship. You can accomplish this either by better understanding your customers' needs or becoming more aggressive in terms of taking the customers' "share of wallet" through better pricing or service. For example, General Motors has successfully developed and sold to car buyers the OnStar system that provides GM with a recurring revenue stream and the car buyer with the

	Existing Products	New Products
Existing Customers	Market Penetration	Cross-Sell (Product Development)
New Customers	Market Development	Start From Scratch (Diversification)

Figure 6.4 Customer–Product Matrix for Revenue Growth Investments (Ansoff's Matrix)

knowledge and security that he or she can have immediate contact with the appropriate personnel in case of an emergency. The advantage of increasing revenues in this way is that you do not need to make extensive investments in product development or customer acquisition; your company is leveraging your existing tangible and intangible assets.

Sell Existing Products to New Customers (Market Development): By selling your existing products and services to new customers, you expand your market opportunities in a growth strategy also known as market development. This approach gives you the benefits of entering a new market without extensive and expensive product development costs, because you already have the product ready to sell. The Gap, for example, has had great success in selling its products to new customers by expanding its retail channels to include a value outlet, Old Navy.

Sell New Products to Existing Customers (Cross-Selling, Product Development): Another revenue growth approach is to cross-sell new products and services to your existing customers. The advantage to this approach is that you already have a relationship with the customers; thus, it should be easier to get them to purchase additional products from you than it was to acquire the customer in the first place. For example, Citibank trains its branch office personnel and supports them with systems to assist in the cross-selling of products and related services.

Sell New Products to New Customers (Starting From Scratch, Diversification): When you sell new products to new customers, you are starting from scratch; you do not have an established customer base or an established product. As we have seen, either factor would make your job easier. This is the most risky type of investment for growing revenue because of the tremendous risks associated with trying to reach new customers while introducing new products. Few companies have been successful at selling new products to new customers. One exception is Circuit City, a major electronics retailer that has successfully built a used-car sales business.

Cable TV and the Value of Customers

Let's take a look at the cable television industry as an example of the value and importance of customers to any business. Cable companies typically own broadcast systems and the cable wiring networks that carry the content, but the value of these systems is inextricably linked to the customers to whom these systems connect. Although competition is increasing with DirecTV and overlapping cable companies in some large metropolitan areas, cable companies mostly act as local monopolies; a company's pool of prospects is limited to households connected to the company's network. At the same time, those customers have few alternatives to the local monopoly cable company.

By the end of 2001, more than 96 percent[1] of U.S. homes had cable service available in their locations. There is no longer much room to grow customers by adding wire to the network, except in the few cases where there are competing cable networks in the same area. At the same time, 70 percent of cable-ready homes had at least basic cable, so there is limited growth potential through new customers. Cable companies have instead focused a great deal of attention on acquiring other companies as a way to increase their customer base. As Table 6.1 shows, cable customers are valued at thousands of dollars each.

Table 6.1   Selected Customer Acquisition Transactions in the Cable Industry

Date	Transaction	# Subscribers	Deal Amount ($Million)	Cost Per Subscriber ($)
February-99	FrontierVision to Adelphia	702,000	$2,100	$2,992
April-99	Harron to Adelphia	300,000	$1,170	$3,900
June-99	Bresnento Charter	690,000	$3,100	$4,493
November-99	Avalon to Charter	260,000	$845	$3,250
November-99	Fanch to Charter	537,000	$2,400	$4,469
November-99	Falcon to Charter	1,000,000	$3,600	$3,600
December-99	Cablevision to Adelphia	306,000	$1,530	$5,000
January-00	Multimedia Cablevision to Cox	522,000	$2,700	$5,172
April-00	Cablevision to AT&T Broadband	232,350	$1,160	$4,993
September-00	Cablevision to Charter	48,600	$171	$3,510
October-00	Media General to Cox	260,000	$1,400	$5,385
February-03	AT&T to Charter	512,000	$1,540	$3,008
February-03	Charter to AT&T Broadband	62,000	$249	$4,016
April-03	AT&T to Comcast	585,000	$1,430	$2,433
November-03	Rogers to GCI	7,300	$19	$2,603
October-03	AT&T Broadband	10,000	$25	$2,500
November-03	AT&T Broadband to Comcast	18,500,000	$410	$2,660

---

1. Cable TV Financial Databook, 2000, p. 10, as presented in *Broadcasting & Cable* (www.broadcastingcable.com).

Although these acquisitions often involve equipment, cable networks, and personnel, the major value driver is the value of the customers. And, to a lesser extent, the value of prospective customers to which the company gets access (noncustomer households along the routes serviced by the company) through the acquisition. At first glance, this seems to be an outrageous amount for a single customer, even if you take the equipment, network, and personnel into consideration. When you look closely at the nature of the customer relationship in the cable industry, it is more reasonable. Because of the local monopolies cable companies typically enjoy, subscribers generally are locked into their cable provider for a long time; thus, the cable company is virtually assured of receiving a long stream of recurring revenues. In addition, cable companies offer a wide range of services, from premium cable channels to high-speed Internet access and phone service, such that annual revenue from some customers can be more than $1,000.

If you were managing a cable company, one of your objectives first would be how to grow revenue per customer. Industry data indicates that the primary revenue and profit driver for the industry is now broadband access. Adding broadband access to a household has a major impact on the value of that customer to the cable company.

The same is true for your company, even though you likely are not in the cable TV business. It is easy enough to see the relationship of a sales-related investment to your customers; if your sales increase, you either have grown your customer base or increased the amount that your customers spend on your products and services. It is not enough to assign a growth rate percentage to sales and multiply it out year by year when you evaluate your investment. You must drill down into your sales projections for more information on your customers. Let's go through the analysis. First, think about which customers you expect to account for the increased sales. To answer this question, think about where the customers to whom you are hoping to sell fit into the customer life cycle in Figure 6.5.

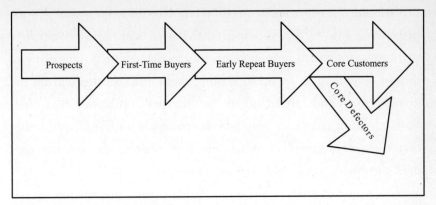

Figure 6.5 Customer Life Cycle

Each of these customer groups has a different set of needs, different purchasing habits, and different revenue value associated with them. When most people think of increasing sales, they think first of sales to new customers (i.e., converting prospects to first-time buyers). As you saw with the Ansoff matrix, new customers do not tell the whole story of revenue growth. Additional sales to additional customers is often an easier way to grow sales. In any case, your customers are not all created equal; some are much more profitable than others, and they should be treated that way.

What Is a Customer Worth?

Let's assume that your company is considering an investment in acquiring new customers. As shown in Table 6.2, there are four questions to consider.

Table 6.2 Four Drill-Down Questions for Determining Customer Value

1. How much do you currently spend on acquiring new customers?
2. How does your overall customer acquisition cost compare to the current proposal?
3. How much does the average customer spend on your products and services?
4. How many customers do you lose every year?

You must answer these questions to determine the value of your customers. Why is this so important? If you don't know what new customers are worth, you have no way to determine how much you should be willing to spend to acquire them and still profit from the investment. Think about all of the Internet companies that went bust pursuing customer acquisition strategies without considering that they were spending much more to acquire those customers than the customers could ever spend on purchases. With this information, you can analyze the impact of customer acquisition investments on value creation—increasing either the number of customers or the average revenue and profitability of a customer to create value. As such, customer value is an important part of the investment process.

Step 1: Determine the Four Determinants of Customer Value

To calculate the value of a customer, you must determine the value of four variables. These are acquisition cost, average annual revenue per customer, average annual attrition rate, and discount rate.

Acquisition Cost: Acquisition cost is how much a company spends to acquire a new customer. To calculate acquisition cost, total all of the money you spend on marketing, advertising, sales calls, and everything else related to getting a new customer. Next, divide this sum by the number of first-time customers you brought in as a result of all of these efforts. This is your average cost of getting a new customer. You can do this across your entire business, or you can use acquisition cost to evaluate the effectiveness of a particular sales effort by using only its associated costs and new customers. Figure 6.6 illustrates the customer acquisition cost calculation.

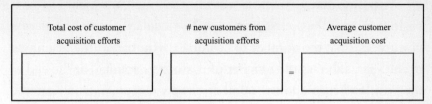

Figure 6.6 Customer Acquisition Cost

Average Annual Revenue Per Customer: Average annual revenue per customer is the annual sales you make to an average customer. There are a few different ways to get this number. If you do not have detailed customer sales information on hand, you can divide your annual sales by the number of customers to get average revenue per customer. If you do have more information available, you should use it to get a better idea of what your typical customers really purchase in a year. With this additional information, you might also be able to look at the buying patterns of different customer groups. If you have a sales database, you can easily get the total purchases of each customer, and you can take the average of those total purchases. The first method is sufficient if you do not have time to look or the right information available. Figure 6.7 illustrates the basic average annual revenue per customer calculation.

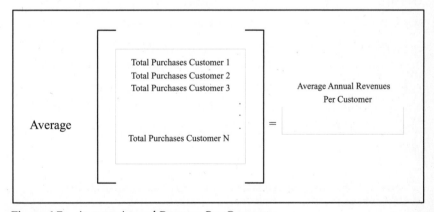

Figure 6.7 Average Annual Revenue Per Customer

Attrition Rate: Attrition rate is the rate at which you lose customers over the course of a year. To calculate attrition rate for a given year, take the number of customers you had at the beginning of the year, subtract the number of customers you had at the end of the year, and then add the number of new customers you acquired during the year. Divide the result by the number of customers at the beginning of the year to get the attrition rate. This process is shown in Figure 6.8.

Calculating attrition rate is easier in some industries than in others, depending largely on the buying habits of your customers and your relationship with them. The effects of attrition are most obvious in cases where your customers make frequent purchases. If your product is something that your customers purchase infrequently, either from you or from a competitor, annual attrition rate isn't a very good way to evaluate your customers. If this is the case, most or all of the value of your customer comes in the initial purchase. To value a customer in this situation, just compare the acquisition cost to the purchase price.

Discount Rate: The discount rate allows you to take into account the time value of money, the fact that a dollar today is worth more than a dollar in the future. The argument over which discount rate to use in a given situation is likely to go on as long as cash flows are discounted, but, as we discussed in an earlier chapter, don't waste too much time worrying about the discount rate. Use your company's cost of capital or pick something conservative, but whatever you do, do not get embroiled with some complicated and ultimately futile exercise in determining cost of capital.

Step 2: Format of Attrition Rate and Discount Rate

The second step is to put the attrition rate and discount rate into a usable form. Attrition rate and discount rate work the same way;

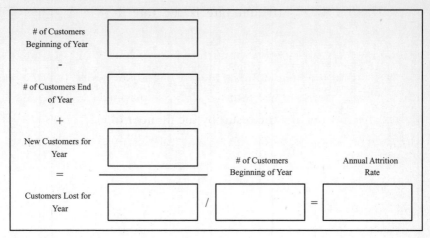

Figure 6.8   Customer Attrition Rate

their effect is cumulative. An easy way to use these rates is to multiply them out ahead of time and then apply the resulting attrition factors and discount factors to your revenue numbers. In each case, it is easier to use the retention rate and the inverse of the discount rate, rather than the raw attrition and discount rates.

Step 3: Calculate Customer Value

You now have everything you need to calculate customer value:

- Customer acquisition cost

- Revenue with attrition: Multiply each year's expected revenue by the attrition factor for each year

- Discounted revenue with attrition: Multiply revenue with attrition by the discount factor for each year

- Discounted revenue with attrition to date

- Net present value to date: Add acquisition cost to the discounted revenue with attrition to date.

Table 6.3 is a spreadsheet template for the process of calculating the value of a customer as just described. By modeling and cal-

	Year 0
Customer Acquisition Cost (C)	C
Average Annual Revenue/ Customer (R)	R
Annual Attrition Rate (A)	A
Discount Rate (D)	D

Year	Year 0	Year 1	Year 2	Year 3	Year 4	Year 5
Annual Attrition		A	A	A	A	A
Annual Retention		$(1-A)$	$(1-A)$	$(1-A)$	$(1-A)$	$(1-A)$
Cumulative Retention Factor		$(1-A)$	$(1-A)^2$	$(1-A)^3$	$(1-A)^4$	$(1-A)^5$
Annual Discount Rate		D	D	D	D	D
Annual Discount Factor		$(1-D)$	$(1-D)$	$(1-D)$	$(1-D)$	$(1-D)$
Cumulative Annual Discount Factor		$(1-D)$	$(1-D)^2$	$(1-D)^3$	$(1-D)^4$	$(1-D)^5$
Customer Acquisition Cost	-C					
Revenue		R	R	R	R	R
Revenue With Attrition		$R(1-A)$	$R(1-A)2$	$R(1-A)3$	$R(1-A)4$	$R(1-A)5$
Discounted Revenue With Attrition (DRA)		$R(1-A)(1-D)$	$R(1-A)^2(1-D)^2$	$R(1-A)^3(1-D)^3$	$R(1-A)^4(1-D)^4$	$R(1-A)^5(1-D)^5$
Discounted Revenue With Attrition To Date (DRATD)		DRA_1	$DRA_1 + DRA_2$	$DRA_1 + DRA_3$	$DRA_1 + DRA_4$	$DRA_1 + DRA_5$
Net Present Value To Date	-C	$-C+DRATD_1$	$-C+DRATD_2$	$-C+DRATD_3$	$-C+DRATD_4$	$-C+DRATD_5$

Customer Acquisition Cost (C)
Average Annual Revenue/ Customer ¤
Annual Attrition Rate (A)
Discount Rate (D)

Year	Year 0	Year 1	Year 2	Year 3	Year 4	Year 5
Annual Attrition						
Annual Retention						
Cumulative Retention Factor						
Annual Discount Rate						
Annual Discount Factor						
Cumulative Annual Discount Factor						
Customer Acquisition Cost						
Revenue						
Revenue With Attrition						
Discounted Revenue With Attrition (DRA)						
Discounted Revenue With Attrition To Date (DRATD)						
Net Present Value To Date						

Table 6.3   Template for Calculating Customer Value

culating customer value, you get several important insights. Revenue to date is the maximum amount you should be willing to spend on a new customer to achieve break-even in the time horizon you specify. You can easily look at the effect of changes in the customer value drivers. You can use this model to see what happens to customer value as customer acquisition cost, revenue per customer, and attrition rate change. Look at scenarios where one or more of the customer acquisition drivers are not as good as you expect to see and determine whether you can get a return on this investment, even if things don't go perfectly.

Summary

Your company will have more successful investments that grow corporate value if it focuses on the execution of those investments prior to making the decision to invest rather than depending primarily on financial analyses and strategic plans. This chapter reviewed execution analysis and discussed the need to drill down in your analysis of prospective investments to confirm that the details (the who, what, when, where, why, and how) are sufficiently covered. By doing so, you can develop a valid road map to follow when executing the investment and ensure a much greater likelihood of success. Another factor to consider is the capital intensity of the investment under consideration. All else being equal, less capital-intense investments provide a greater return at a lower risk. As part of the execution analysis, you must also consider the sequencing of the resources and the trade-offs that your company must make with changes in resources, time, and scope. Finally, you must assess the impact any investment will have on your customers, and know the value of your customers to make decisions on customer acquisition investments. This chapter gave you the tools to analyze execution, capital intensity, and customer value, factors that together can greatly improve the chances that your investment will be a success.

Following the Roadmap

Let's consider Fresh Breeze and walk through an example using the Roadmap. The R&D laboratory at Fresh Breeze has developed a new detergent that, in the view of its marketing people, has supreme cleaning power. Managers at the company now must decide how to "productize" and launch the product. Although the product has been developed in the laboratory, managers must answer the who, what, when, where, why, and how questions, the details of the investment that will allow them to execute the investment successfully.

Fresh Breeze must run a sales and marketing campaign that not only drives demand from consumers, but also gets retailers to carry the product. Depending on Fresh Breeze's manufacturing capacity, it might also need to temporarily outsource the manufacturing of the new product to ensure that it is on shelves in time for the start of the consumer promotional campaign. Fresh Breeze should ask these questions through every stage of the investment, from the laboratory to store shelves, and, more importantly, into homes. Even though the product has already been developed in the laboratory, there are significant challenges ahead and many questions that need an answer before the investment should proceed.

The timing and sequence of the investment must be carefully coordinated. It could prove to be a real disaster if the marketing and sales campaign went into full swing before the product was actually available to consumers, or if promotions were launched before any retailers agreed to carry the new product. In addition, the company would be well advised to test the product in a few selected markets before it commits all of its resources to a full-fledged product launch. Timing and sequence are obviously critical.

When Fresh Breeze applies the "How many yeses?" question to the new detergent, it finds that there are several levels (the channels of distribution) that must be convinced before the consumer even has a chance to buy the product. In contrast, think of how much simpler this particular challenge would be if Fresh Breeze promoted and sold products directly to end users, such as through direct mail.

Fresh Breeze also must determine the capital intensity of this investment. This means projecting the working capital that will be necessary to launch and grow the new product successfully. The company's working capital analysis must take the competitive environment into consideration; for example, it must compete effectively with the promotions and pricing of other, better established brands.

In addition, Fresh Breeze must consider the capital asset requirements of the investment. These might have an even more significant effect on capital intensity than working capital. If Fresh Breeze has limited capacity to make new products because its current production facilities are running near capacity utilization, it must invest in new factories and equipment. If the product is a success, what had been a relatively low-intensity capital investment will soon require a great deal of capital investment.

Finally, Fresh Breeze must consider the effect that the new detergent product will have on its customers. Will the new detergent cannibalize Fresh Breeze's other detergent brands, or will it convince customers of its competitors to defect to the new brand? How does the quality and marketing image of the new product line up with Fresh Breeze's overall market image and the image consumers have about the company and its products?

Although Fresh Breeze faces tremendous challenges, a detailed analysis of its execution plans will make its investment road smoother and will greatly increase its chances of success.

Value of a Fresh Breeze Customer

Fresh Breeze's direct customers are the wholesalers and retailers who distribute and sell its products to other businesses and consumers. It is easy enough for Fresh Breeze to determine which of these accounts provide it with the most revenues and profits. The company must not focus solely on its direct customers, the wholesalers and distributors; these customers act only as middle men between Fresh Breeze and its ultimate customers, other businesses and individual consumers who purchase Fresh Breeze products in retail stores. When these customers shop, they have a wide variety of competitors from which to choose; Fresh Breeze does not enjoy the same captive audience as cable TV companies. To encourage customers to try and then stick with its products, Fresh Breeze employs a combination of coupons, promotions, and other incentives; product displays; careful product placement in specific retail channels; and marketing and advertising efforts. This creates a complex situation for analysis, but Fresh Breeze managers must nonetheless understand the average revenues each new and existing customer generates and the cost of the sales, marketing, and advertising efforts relative to the sales they generate.

Average Annual Revenues Per Customer: Because it works closely with its retail and wholesale customers, Fresh Breeze was able to get data on customer purchases. From this data, Fresh Breeze estimates that about 25 million consumer customers purchased its products in 2002. This includes everyone from one-time buyers (who purchased a single Fresh Breeze product on a single occasion due to a promotion, convenience, or some other trial and will likely never purchase another product) to loyal, core customers (who make frequent purchases of many Fresh Breeze products each year). It does not make sense to treat these disparate customer types the same for anything but the most basic analysis, so Fresh Breeze divided its customers into four tiers.

Tier 1 is the core customer group. Tier 2 consists of regular customers who only purchase a fraction of the Fresh Breeze products that Tier 1 customers do. Tier 3 consists of irregular customers who occasionally purchase Fresh Breeze products out of convenience or because of particular promotions. Tier 4 customers are one-time purchasers. In addition to its tiering system, Fresh Breeze divides its customers by the combinations of products they buy. For example, some customers buy only Fresh Breeze personal cleaning products, whereas others buy personal cleaning products and laundry care products. Still others buy personal cleaning, laundry care, and air freshener products. Customers who purchase more than one Fresh Breeze product line tend to be more loyal customers. Therefore, more of these multiproduct customers tend to fall into Tier 1. At Fresh Breeze, just like at your company, all customers are not equal. It is important to be able to classify your customers according to their value.

Average customers, across all tiers and product types, spend an average of $44.13 per year. Because Fresh Breeze tracks revenue per customer by a four-tiered grouping system and by the product segments from which customers purchase, it should use this more detailed data to target its customer acquisition strategies to the most profitable customers, Tier 1 customers who buy more than one Fresh Breeze product line.

Acquisition Cost: Fresh Breeze spent a total of $193 million on sales activities in 2002, and the net customer base increased to 25 million from 23.8 million during the year. During 2002, the company also lost an estimated 3.7 million customers (15.5 percent of its 2001 customer base; see the discussion of attrition rate later). Thus, the total increase in customers was 4.9 million (25 million customers at the end of the year less 23.8 million customers at the beginning of the year less 3.7 million customers lost equals 4.9 million new customers). Dividing $193 million by 4.9 million, you can see that Fresh Breeze spends an average of $39.40 to acquire a new customer. This figure is useful in calculating the average net present value of a Fresh Breeze customer, as well as to provide a baseline comparison to proposed investments.

Attrition Rate: Fresh Breeze experiences different attrition rates for its different customer groups. Not surprisingly, customers who purchase more of Fresh Breeze's products tend to be more loyal to Fresh Breeze products. In addition, customers who purchase several types of Fresh Breeze products also have more of an affinity for the brand. The average overall attrition rate is 15.5 percent.

Discount Rate: Fresh Breeze has an average cost of capital of 10 percent; this is the discount rate it will use in its customer value calculation.

Calculating the Value of a Customer

Applying these estimates to the template in Table 6.3, the five-year net present value of a customer is $73.76, given the current average customer acquisition cost of $39.40. The present value of the five-year revenue stream from a customer is $123.24 as shown in Table 6.4.

What do these numbers mean? First, Fresh Breeze's current customer acquisition practices overall are profitable. In theory, the company should be willing to spend as much as $123.24 to acquire a customer, which would yield a five-year net present value of $0. In practice, Fresh Breeze would target less expensive customer acquisition investments. The time horizon is extremely important in this analysis. Note that after two years, a customer's discounted

Table 6.4 Fresh Breeze Five-Year Net Present Value of a Customer

	Year 0	Year 1	Year 2	Year 3	Year 4	Year 5
Customer Acquisition Cost	$39.40					
Average Annual Revenue/ Customer	$44.13					
Annual Attrition Rate	15.5%					
Discount Rate	10.0%					
Year	Year 0	Year 1	Year 2	Year 3	Year 4	Year 5
Retention Factor	100.0%	84.5%	71.4%	60.3%	51.0%	43.1%
Discount Factor	100.0%	90.0%	90.0%	90.0%	90.0%	90.0%
Customer Acquisition Cost	-$39.40					
Revenue	$0.00	$44.13	$44.13	$44.13	$44.13	$44.13
Revenue With Attrition	$0.00	$37.29	$31.51	$26.63	$22.50	$19.01
Discounted Revenue With Attrition	$0.00	$33.56	$28.36	$23.96	$20.25	$17.11
Discounted Revenue With Attrition To Date	$0.00	$33.56	$61.92	$85.88	$106.13	$123.24
Net Present Value To Date	**-$39.40**	**-$5.84**	**$22.52**	**$46.48**	**$66.73**	**$83.84**

revenue stream is worth only $62.92, which under the current customer acquisition conditions has a net present value of $12.44.

Because Fresh Breeze has detailed, segmented data available, it would be well-served to calculate customer value for each customer group it was interested in, and match customer acquisition investments with the most appropriate customer target segments as efficiently as possible.

7

ONGOING
MANAGEMENT

Plan the work and work the plan.

A maxim at IBM

You have taken your investment all the way from an idea or concept to the cusp of reality following the Business Investment Roadmap. You began with the preliminary analysis, made the decision to proceed, assessed the impact of the investment on your company, considered risk factors and developed a risk mitigation plan, and thoroughly considered the execution of your investment. You have peeled the onion back further and further and have reached the point where the investment has received the green light. Figure 7.1 illustrates how far you have come.

Is it time to declare victory? Take a much-needed vacation? Move onto something else? Absolutely not! You still have a long

175

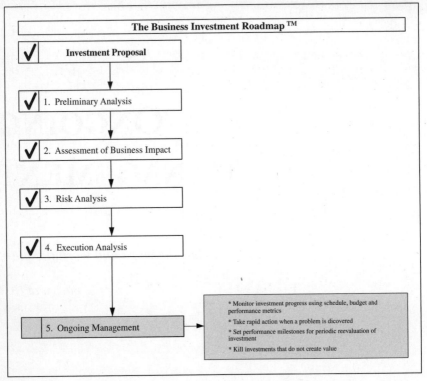

Figure 7.1   Decision Route: The Business Investment Roadmap:
Ongoing Management

way to go to ensure that the investment is successful in growing corporate value. Like the captain of the ship that has left its port, you need to navigate the investment through the inevitable troubled waters until it has reached its ultimate destination of creating value for your company. Like the captain of the ship at sea, you need to be on the lookout for changes in the weather patterns and other conditions that require a shift in your original course (the execution), as well as closely monitor the ship's internal gauges to ensure that everything is functioning properly and according to expectations. You need to monitor the progress of your investment closely throughout its implementation, take decisive action when problems occur, and reevaluate or even kill your investment if its performance is irreparably compromised, or the assumptions underlying your projections of how it will create corporate value change significantly.

This chapter provides an overview of the last element of the Business Investment Roadmap, ongoing management. The objective is to provide you with a set of tools that will help you keep your investment on course so that you can create corporate value. Starting with a cross-country road trip as an analogy for the ongoing management of an investment, this chapter describes how to choose and use schedule, budget, and performance metrics to monitor your investment's progress and to detect problems as early as possible.

The chapter also discusses the importance of developing your own internal gauges for tracking progress. One approach that has been particularly successful is earned value analysis (EVA), a tool originally developed by the U.S. Department of Defense that allows you to simultaneously track schedule, budget, and performance. EVA is only one of many tools you can use to track performance. The key is that your company needs a disciplined and consistent approach that it can use when monitoring investments and for taking actions when and if necessary. There is an example of earned value analysis in the "Following the Roadmap" section at the end of the chapter.

Cross-Country Road Trip

Imagine that you are about to drive from Los Angeles to Boston to take a new position in the company's Boston office. You have mapped out in detail the costs, the resources needed, the time, the roads, and even some of the places you want to visit along the way: Las Vegas, Mount Rushmore and the Badlands, Nashville, and Chicago. You expect the trip to take 10 days and cost $1,500. You leave Los Angeles and head east, with a plan to be in South Dakota by Day 4. When Day 4 arrives, however, you are only in Denver. You made much slower progress than you had expected. Car trouble requiring expensive repairs contributed to the delay. The bigger reason you are behind, however, was a longer-than-anticipated stop in Las Vegas, during which you managed to gamble away a significant portion of your trip money.

After the first four days, here is where you stand: You are in Denver rather than South Dakota. Given your initial 10-day, $1,500 trip budget, you should have spent $600 through the first four days of your trip ($150 per day). Instead, you have spent $900. You have a problem: You are behind in time and over budget, and you have not met your performance milestones.

Your original travel plan needs some major revisions. The new plan must take into account your current situation and your final objectives. You do have a number of alternatives in how you can correct the course of your trip and acknowledge the reality of your new situation. You have been driving at the speed limit so far, but you could drive faster, especially on some of the wide-open western highways. However, if you drive faster, you will spend more money on gas. You have been driving 8 hours per day; you could increase your daily driving time to 10 hours. This will also increase your daily cost of gasoline, but it might not affect your total budget overall, because you would have to cover those miles anyway. Alternatively, you could extend the total time of your trip from 10 to 12 days, and you could continue driving at the same speed and for the same amount of time per day as before. This would also increase the cost of your trip, due to additional meals and nights in motels. These three alternatives all amount to changing the schedule of your trip.

Another option is to cut some of the sightseeing stops out of your trip. In doing so, you save time because you avoid stops and detours from the main route. You also save money because you are not paying for admission to Mt. Rushmore or the Grand Old Opry, and you save on gas money because you have cut some detours out of the trip. In other words, you can cut scope from your trip plan.

You could adjust your budget for the remainder of the trip. You could save money by cutting scope as just discussed. You could also increase the amount you plan to spend on the trip. For example, you could maintain your $150 daily allowance for the rest of the trip, which would mean that at the end, you would have spent more than the original $1,500. You could also cut down your daily budget so that your total budget remains the same. All of these actions involve changing your budget.

The interrelatedness of schedule, scope, and budget is now obvious, and it is likely familiar to you from your experiences at work and at home. In facing the dilemma of revising your travel plan in this example, you are dealing with the iron triangle of schedule, scope, and budget discussed earlier in this book. You have to make a choice sooner or later, because you know that going forward with the initial execution plan will no longer work. It is time to rethink the investment and the execution plan. This is part of ongoing management.

One of the questions you should ask is how you deviated from your travel plan. When did the trip get off track? Your extended stay cost you an additional $100 over your daily budget, and the stopover put you behind by at least 20 percent (2 days on a 10-day trip). Similarly, the car repairs cost you $200 and some additional delay. Each of these events effectively required a change in the execution plan in regard to schedule, scope, or budget. Simply ignoring them when they happened or assuming that you would make up the difference later on does not work in this situation, and will not work with most investments.

Another question you might have is what you can do about the cost and time overruns. You could cut your daily budget for food, hotels, and so on from the planned $150 to $100 per day to maintain the original total budget for the trip ($900 already spent, plus

$100 per day for the six remaining days). To catch up on time, you would need to cut out some sightseeing and drive through the night for two nights to compensate for the lost time in Las Vegas.

It is much better that you realized you were over budget and behind schedule on the fourth day of the trip rather than near the end of the journey. Although none of your options are great, you can still take action to get your trip back on track. If you didn't realize you were off schedule and over budget until the eighth day, when you ran out of cash in Cleveland, it would be too late to take corrective action. No matter how fast you drove or how conservative you were with your spending, you could not get there in 10 days and for $1,500. Again, it is always better to recognize problems early and take corrective action when you still have time and resource options you can reconfigure.

Now assume that you must be in Boston within 10 days or the new job will be given to someone else. Because of this tight schedule, you develop some milestones. Although the original plan called for you to be in Denver by the end of Day 2, you have to be there by Day 4 to have any chance at arriving in Boston within the 10-day limit. Similarly, although you originally planned to be in Chicago in six days, you must now be there by the end of Day 7, or you will not be able to complete your trip in time. Given this scenario, you made it to Denver in four days, so you are behind schedule, but you still made the performance milestone that allows you to continue. If you are in St. Louis and not Chicago at the end of Day 8, you might as well turn around and head back to California, because you cannot make up enough time to get to Boston by the deadline.

In a third case, assume that you made even better progress than you planned. After four days, you have crossed the border into Minnesota. You are ahead of schedule, and you have spent less money than you had budgeted. At this rate, you might make it to Boston in eight days, with a couple hundred dollars to spare!

Things appear to be going splendidly, until you check your voice mail when you stop for coffee and find out that your position has been eliminated. You are no longer needed in Boston. You have no choice but to turn around and head back to Los Angeles.

Lessons From the Trip

These travel scenarios provide some important lessons to keep in mind in the ongoing management of your company's investments:

1. Monitor your progress using several metrics, including time, budget, and performance.

2. Take rapid action when you discover a problem, and the sooner you discover and react to a problem, the better.

3. Set performance milestones that give you periodic opportunities to reevaluate an investment.

4. You must be prepared to kill your investment entirely if the investment is no longer valuable.

Monitor Progress Using Time, Cost, and Performance Metrics

An important part of the investment evaluation process is the development of metrics you can use to assess its progress, specifically time, cost, and performance metrics. Together, these metrics can give you a pretty good idea of how well your investment is doing, but you cannot get an accurate picture without measuring all three. Any one of these metrics, however carefully and accurately measured, is not of much use in evaluating the progress of an investment.

Let's go back to the driving example for a moment. What if you tracked only the time it took you to drive across the country (schedule), without regard either to how much money you were spending (budget) or to any of the sightseeing stops you planned to make (performance milestones)? You could very well end your trip thousands of dollars over budget, without stopping at any of the places you wanted to see along the way. Similarly, if you only paid attention to your budget, with no attention to schedule or landmarks, you would be unlikely either to make it to Boston in the requisite 10 days or to see any of the sights. Finally, if you were only focused on your sightseeing visits, your trip could take weeks and cost thousands of dollars. You should note that by choosing only two of these three parameters to measure, you still have great potential for trouble in the one you ignore. So carefully track all three, or ignore them at your peril.

Time and cost are pretty straightforward metrics; you probably track schedules and budgets already. Most companies do. Performance measurement—what the investment has accomplished for the amount of time and money that has been expended on it—is a bit trickier. At a minimum, you should judge performance by the milestones you set, but you also need a way to measure quality and other parameters directly related to the investment. Think of industrial manufacturing in East Germany before the reunification of Germany. The managers at the plants usually met their production unit quotas, but the quality and reliability of the products they produced were generally poor.

Closer to home, consider some of the failures in ERP software implementations that have been noted in the popular press and business books. In many of these implementations the systems integration firms bill more on the basis of time and percentage of budget (often called time and materials billing, or T&M) rather than on what has been accomplished. Inevitably, many of these investments ultimately cost much more than expected, finish late, and require a reduction in scope. What's particularly astonishing is that companies often wake up to discover, for example, that they have spent 75 percent of the budget in the allotted time (the ERP system should have been implemented by that date) with much less of the needed work completed.

Obviously, these situations are often due to more than just actions or lack of actions by the systems integration firms; companies often change what they want as they learn more about what the software can do. Similarly, companies—particularly large, complex organizations—often underfund organizational change that enables the ERP systems to work effectively (a risk discussed in an earlier chapter). The important point is that if performance had been measured along the way, then the systems integration firms and the companies could have made changes in budget, schedule, or scope much earlier and mitigated the risk of major contentious problems later.

Kaplan and Norton begin their book *The Balanced Scorecard* by asking the reader to imagine a conversation with an airline pilot who uses just one gauge to guide the plane.[1] Obviously, you, as the passenger, would not feel comfortable with the pilot using just a single gauge; flying a plane requires a lot of data of different types. Their point is that companies need a comprehensive set of performance measures that provide a framework for a strategic measurement and management system.[2] There are also several other general management-level approaches for measuring performance of companies, such as the performance pyramid.

---

1. Robert S. Kaplan and David P. Norton. *The Balanced Scorecard* (Boston: Harvard Business School Press, 1996).
2. Ibid. p. 2.

The key issue in developing useful metrics is to make certain that they have a direct impact on growing corporate value. Macro or general-level performance metrics clearly add value, but from the perspective of day-to-day execution (i.e., moving from strategy to financial returns), it is critical to measure cost, budget, and performance.

At General Electric, one of the world's largest and most highly valued companies, some managers use a "digital dashboard" that reports the status of several important company operations in green, yellow, and red on their desktops. The colors indicate the level of concern for potential problems, and the specific metrics on each manager's desktop are tailored to his or her individual needs and job responsibilities. One manager's desktop might include, for example, daily order rates and inventory levels.

Although you probably do not have your own "digital dashboard," you do need to develop clear, unambiguous performance metrics for tracking investments. Do not be content with simply having to wait for the "completed" product or service. Instead, work with investment team proponents to determine specific milestones that are linked with value creation. Tie the allocation of company resources to the investment according to those milestones. If milestones are not met, it might be best to exit that investment option and devote the company's limited resources to other investments that have been more successful in reaching their milestones.

Unfortunately, unlike your road trip from Los Angeles to Boston, where the milestones are clearly marked along the highway, defining clear and precise milestones with most of your company's investments will be a more difficult process. You can make your job much easier if you work directly with the investment's major proponents and team members. Allow the closest people to the investment (and consequently the ones who understand it best) to develop the milestones and link them to the resources they need.

Earned Value Analysis: Measuring Performance and Taking Action

More than 40 years ago, the U.S. Department of Defense developed a formal methodology to help evaluate its investment in the Minuteman missile program. The methodology, called earned value analysis (EVA), was based on 35 factors that formed the basis for assessing progress; the resulting calculation was called earned value. The process of tracking and evaluating these factors, particularly in the days before the use of real-time desktop computing, was extremely tedious. For a long time, EVA was confined primarily to investments made by the military, public works, and some large-scale private investments. Nevertheless, the process has endured and is now a critical part of the professional practice of project management.

Tracking performance in a disciplined and consistent way has moved beyond the necessity of monitoring the Department of Defense's 35 factors, the tedium of manual calculations, and the application of earned value primarily to military or large-scale investments. Fueled primarily by computing power, today nearly every project management software package, including Microsoft Project, can calculate earned value. In addition, the EVA methodology has been refined and simplified, so there are fewer variables to track. In its current state, EVA, or even more simplified approaches based on EVA that are tailored to your company, can be a valuable tool in the ongoing management of your investments.

Earned value or other more simplified approaches tailored to your company will enable you to track schedule, cost, and performance simultaneously. You can and should use earned value or your customized approach to measure earned value before, during, and, in certain situations, even after investments are completed. In this way, you will be able to link performance with time and expenditures, starting in the early stages of the investment. You will also be able to discover problems and take rapid action before small problems grow larger. EVA and similar approaches are tools for assessing the efficiency and effectiveness of your investment along the way as well as after the fact. In the process, you earn value by completing a portion of the total work needed for a successful investment.

Alternatives to Earned Value

EVA is by no means the only tool available to you for tracking and managing investments. As noted earlier, your company might want to develop an alternative that is simpler to use and apply because it is customized specifically to your needs. The methodology you use is not as important as the fact that it will enable you regularly to track the progress of your investments relative to expected milestones, costs, schedule, and other critical metrics.

The critical benefit of being able to access the information to assess performance in meeting objectives is the ability to act quickly and, thereby, gain a strategic advantage. You might wonder what is meant by "regularly." Here is the bottom line: If more granular (increasingly lower levels of detail) tracking improves the likelihood that your investments succeed, then that is your answer. Keep in mind that although General Electric's "digital dashboard" deals primarily with real-time data, this is usually unnecessary for most companies. In most situations you will do just fine with weekly, semimonthly, or even monthly data. The granularity required will depend on the nature of your investment; daily performance tracking is much more important with an investment that lasts a year in duration than one that lasts a week.

Killing Investments: Be Prepared to Stop

Another advantage of having an ongoing management system is that it gives you the knowledge and insight to decide that enough is enough. Many investments should be stopped partway through for a variety of reasons, even if they have succeeded in achieving schedule and cost milestones. Every investment is part of your company's portfolio of investments; not all investments will be successful and create value. Instead, as noted in an earlier chapter, consider each investment as an option and the major milestones as decision stages to proceed (i.e., devote additional resources) or end (i.e., devote resources to other investments that have more promising returns). Going back to your cross-country trip, the elimination of the position in Boston meant the end of the trip, even though it was ahead of schedule. It no longer made sense, given the new information that the job was no longer available. You will most likely face situations with some frequency in which you need to terminate investments.

There will be times when you need to evaluate an investment when it reaches a milestone on time and on budget, and you still have to decide not to exercise your option by devoting more resources to it. Changes in technology, approvals by regulatory authorities, and price wars from competitors are examples of factors that require you to reassess and, if appropriate, kill an investment and move on with other investment opportunities.

Stop if the Value Is Not There

You also need to be prepared to stop investing if milestones are not reached within the expected schedule and budget. Deciding to kill an investment is often a difficult, or even an emotional decision. Sometimes it means walking away and acknowledging failure. No one wants to be associated with failure. You might be familiar with the statement, "Success has many fathers, failure has none", which some have attributed to President John F. Kennedy. Typically, the proponents of the investment and others involved will seek to reverse the decision because of their own attachment to it and personal interests. However, if an investment is not meeting the agreed-on milestones and there is not sufficient justification for changing the milestones and redoing the execution plan, you are obligated to kill it to meet your responsibilities as a manager. As part of the death notice, you should ask proponents of the investment to salvage value from what has been invested so far; there might be assets that can be reused elsewhere in the company or sold for something more than "fire sale" prices.

Summary

Ongoing management is a critical part of ensuring that your company's investments help to grow corporate value. The effort of ongoing management includes a prior and ex post facto evaluation and taking appropriate action to ensure success. An important part of ongoing management is developing and applying a set of consistent metrics for evaluating progress. These metrics should, at a minimum, cover time, budget, and performance. The hard part, of course, is developing and using an operational definition of performance; you need to work closely with the proponents of the investments to define performance and other metrics. Make sure that the metrics you use are directly linked to the key value drivers of your business and your customers.

One methodology for linking performance with time and budgets is EVA. This methodology can help you to recognize issues as early as possible, before they turn into major problems. The key is to use EVA or other methodologies customized to fit your company's specific needs as tools to assess how your investment is doing. If necessary, take corrective actions, up to and including terminating the investment entirely to free up resources for other investments with a greater chance of success.

Following the Roadmap

Fresh Breeze has decided to invest in a major software upgrade. It is specifically interested in reducing inventory levels, filling orders more quickly, and streamlining its procurement process. The investment in the software and the configuration is expected to cost $6 million and take one year to complete. For simplicity's sake, assume that Fresh Breeze's investment calls for an equal amount of the total work to be completed each month (8.3 percent of the total budget) and that costs will be equal each month ($500,000 per month for 12 months for a total budget of $6 million). If the investment proceeds according to plan, Fresh Breeze will complete 8.3 percent in Month 1 (8.3 percent of the duration) at a cost of $500,000 (8.3 percent of the total investment). Let's apply these baseline numbers with the EVA terminology, specifically, the following terms:

- Budgeted cost of work scheduled (BCWS) is the portion of the budget that corresponds to the work that has been scheduled to be completed so far. In the baseline Fresh Breeze scenario, BCWS through Month 1 is $500,000, through Month 2, $1,000,000, and so on.

- Budgeted cost of work performed (BCWP) is the portion of the investment that corresponds to the work that has been scheduled to have been done so far. In the baseline case, the BCWP is also $500,000 in Month 1, $1,000,000 in Month 2, and so on.

- Actual cost of work performed (ACWP) is the amount of money that has been spent so far in performing the work. For the baseline of Fresh Breeze's investment, ACWP is $500,000 in Month 1, $1,000,000 in Month 2, and so on.

- Cost variance (CV) = BCWP − ACWP is the overall difference between the budgeted cost and the actual cost of the work performed. Negative values indicate that the company is over budget; in the baseline Fresh Breeze case, there is no CV.

- Schedule variance (SV) = BCWP − BCWS is the difference between the budgeted cost of the work performed and the budgeted cost of the work scheduled. In the Fresh Breeze baseline case, there is no SV.

- Cost performance index (CPI) = BCWP/ACWP is the ratio of the budgeted cost to the actual cost of the work performed. Values less than one indicate that the company is over budget, values over one indicate that the company is under its budget, and a value of one, as in the Fresh Breeze baseline case, means that the company is on budget.

- Schedule performance index (SPI) = BCWP/BCWS is the ratio of the budgeted cost of work performed and the budgeted cost of work scheduled. If the SPI is greater than one, the company is ahead of schedule; when the SPI is less than one it means that the company is behind schedule; and a value of one, as in the Fresh Breeze baseline case, means that the company is on schedule.

Very few investments go exactly according to the original execution plan, and this one is no exception. In Month 1, Fresh Breeze keeps on schedule, so that BCWP is $500,000. The work performed was $100,000 more than the budget specified, however, so that ACWP is $600,000. As a result, there is a CV of $100,000, and a CPI of 0.833, meaning that the company is over budget. The SV, however, is 0, and the SPI is 1; the company is on schedule (see Table 7.1).

Fresh Breeze should be concerned about the fact that it is already over budget by 20 percent ($600,000/$500,000), depending on the reasons for the higher-than-expected costs. If this trend were to continue, the company would be done in the same 12 months as the original plan, but it would cost $7.2 million, rather than the original $6 million budget. The CPI and SPI ratios provide an easy way to rapidly determine what is happening. Because CPI is less than 1, the BCWP is less than its actual cost, and, therefore, the company is over budget. The smaller the CPI ratio, the bigger the problem of cost overruns. SPI works the same way. An SPI of less than one means that the work performed is less than the work scheduled, and, again, the smaller the number, the further behind is the work.

If the company had not been tracking schedule, budget, and performance together, it might not have realized that it was over budget until much later. Because only 10 percent of the budget has

Table 7.1 Fresh Breeze Software Implementation, Earned Value Analysis Month 1

		Month 1
Budgeted Cost of Work Scheduled	BCWS	$500,000
Budgeted Cost of Work Performed	BCWP	$500,000
Actual Cost of Work Performed	ACWP	$600,000
Cost Variance	CV	-$100,000
Schedule Variance	SV	$0
Cost Performance Index	CPI	0.83
Schedule Performance Index	SPI	1

been committed so far, Fresh Breeze has ample opportunity to take steps to get back on track. If, on the other hand, this trend had continued but had not been picked up on until Month 6, the company would be $600,000 over budget. In this case, with 60 percent of the budget already spent and 50 percent of the work completed, there is much less opportunity for the company to make adjustments and get back on track.

The company ran into some additional problems in Month 2, as shown in Table 7.2. Not only did it fall behind schedule (by 20 percent for Month 2, 10 percent overall), but the original investment is continuing to cost more ($600,000 in Month 2, $1,200,000 overall). As the EVA indicates, the company is now slightly behind schedule but, in addition, it is significantly over budget. If the company continues with the same efficiency as it has had so far, this aspect of the investment will take 13 months but cost $8 million, rather than the original $6 million budgeted.

Table 7.2   Fresh Breeze Software Implementation, Earned Value Analysis, Months 1–2

	Month 1	Month 2	To Date
BCWS	$500,000	$500,000	$1,000,000
BCWP	$500,000	$400,000	$900,000
ACWP	$600,000	$600,000	$1,200,000
CV = BCWP-ACWP	-$100,000	-$200,000	-$300,000
SV = BCWP-BCWS	$0	-$100,000	-$100,000
CPI = BCWP/ACWP	0.83	0.67	0.75
SPI = BCWP/BCWS	1.00	0.80	0.90
% TOTAL WORK SCHEDULED	8.30%	8.3%	16.7%
% TOTAL BUDGET SCHEDULED	8.30%	8.3%	16.7%
% TOTAL WORK PERFORMED	8.30%	6.7%	15.0%
% TOTAL BUDGET SPENT	10.00%	10.0%	20.0%
ESTIMATED TIME AT TO DATE EFFICIENCY ((BCWS/BCWP) X PROJECT LENGTH)			13 months
ESTIMATED COST AT TO DATE EFFICIENCY ((ACWP/BCWP) X PROJECT BUDGET))			$8 Million

The company's investment is now in significant danger, mainly due to cost overruns. Luckily, it is early enough that Fresh Breeze can do something about it, such as increase the budget, increase the time needed to complete the investment, or cut scope. If it does any of these things, however, it then needs to reevaluate the entire investment. For example, if it decides to increase the budget, it needs to determine what the value of the investment is if it costs $8 million, instead of $6 million. Lengthening the schedule might also affect the value of the overall investment. If Fresh Breeze decides to cut scope to reduce the budget and time required to complete the investment, it needs to reevaluate the value of the reduced functionality relative to the new expected costs. The company might even choose to abandon the investment if it appears that there is no way to get it back on track and create future value.

Whatever Fresh Breeze decides to do, the critical point is that its use of earned value gives it a way to find out about problems early on in the process, when they could still be fixed. Otherwise, it might have been some time before the company realized its investment was in trouble, which might have come too late for it to do anything about it.

8

NOW IS THE TIME

The longest journey begins with the first step.

Chairman Mao quoting Lao Tzu

Walk into any bookstore, open any magazine, scan any directory, and you'll find a plethora of books, articles, or consultants that offer "solutions" for making your company better. You are near the end of this book, and you might still wonder, "How is the Business Investment Roadmap different, and how can it be effective in helping my company make better investments?" We offer three important justifications for adoption of the Business Investment Roadmap. First, you should use the Business Investment Roadmap to adjust your thinking to move on *and* move out of the recession mindset. It is time to open the corporate checkbook and make investments to grow the value of your company. Every company needs to grow to survive, and every manager needs to think beyond the next quarter or next year. The investments you choose or pass over now will be a major factor in the success or failure of your company in the future. Minding the checkbook is good, but keeping the checkbook glued shut while you and other managers are fighting the war of the last recession is bad for both your company and your own career. As we have described throughout this book, many companies made and continue to make horrendous investment decisions. Although there will always be mistakes and misguided investment efforts, you cannot afford to let the mistakes of the past define your company's future.

Second, the Business Investment Roadmap gives you a bridge across the execution gap between grand strategies and visions and the metrics associated with financial analysis. Too many companies have made investment decisions based primarily on "strategic visions" and financial analysis with questionable assumptions and numbers. The inevitable result has been tremendous losses in shareholder value and finger pointing as everyone seek to place blame on everyone else. The Roadmap is the bridge you can use to cross the gap and achieve successful investments.

Third, the Business Investment Roadmap does not require a significant investment in organizational change. Much of the Roadmap simply makes intuitive sense; it is not particularly complex, difficult, or expensive to implement. Instead, your call to action is to apply the Roadmap incrementally to what you are already doing. Most managers already have enough difficulty getting through their day-to-day responsibilities without adding to them by trying to implement a complex new methodology for making and managing investments. There is no complex new methodology here; rather, this book offers the starting point for your own interesting and exciting journey. Now is the time to start on your way!

Boiled down to its essentials, the Business Investment Roadmap is an organized methodology that supports and enhances the idea that what matters in business investments is a mastery of business basics, as Noria, Joyce, and Roberson wrote in a *Harvard Business Review* article entitled, "What Really Works." They wrote that "New management techniques heat up and fizzle out—seemingly overnight. Most techniques have no direct impact on superior business performance. What does? Mastery of business basics."[1]

The Business Investment Roadmap

This book laid out the Business Investment Roadmap for you as a step-by-step approach for evaluating and executing investments, called the Decision Route. The Decision Route and the Roadmap it creates is a guide to help you to develop and apply a mastery of business basics to corporate investments. The Roadmap as it is described here will get you started on the road to smarter, more successful, and more profitable business investments, but it is not a standard, off-the-rack approach. Every company has its own particular needs and objectives. You should use the material from the book, but use it as a beginning, not an end. Get others involved and customize the Roadmap for your company's unique needs, constraints, and opportunities.

---

1. Nitin Nohria, William Joyce, and Bruce Roberson. "What Really Works," *Harvard Business Review OnPoint*, No. 4260, July 2003.

The foundation for the Roadmap is grounded in many of the same tools that you already use in your day-to-day work. The key is in how they are combined with other tools and structured into a consistent but flexible methodology. Consider the Business Investment Roadmap Decision Route and how it applies to your company. Figure 8.1 summarizes the Decision Route.

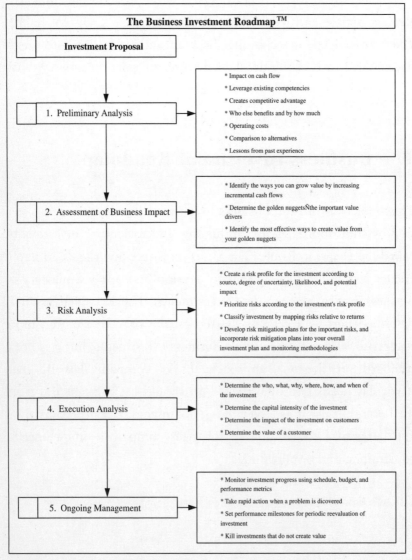

Figure 8.1   Decision Route: The Business Investment Roadmap

Preliminary Analysis

The preliminary analysis is the starting point when evaluating investments using the Business Investment Roadmap. The key objective of the preliminary analysis is to get you to approach each potential investment from a broader perspective than the pure financial analysis that is normally used. How many dollars and how much time could your company have saved if it had followed these steps? The early part of the book asked you questions about how your company evaluates and executes investments. Think about how that discussion might be different if someone at your company had been asking the six key questions in the preliminary analysis.

The preliminary analysis asks you about cash flows, the competencies of your company and its capability to leverage these competencies in the investment, the investment's ability to help your company build a competitive advantage, other beneficiaries of the investment outside your company, the long-term commitment required by your company, the next best alternatives you have to the investment, and the lessons you and your company have learned from the past. If you force the proponents of the investment to answer these questions, it will enable you to determine the viability of the investment quickly. These questions also provide a useful reality check that can often help you minimize investments that reduce corporate value and waste valuable management time.

Business Impact

Think back to the relationship of razor blades to profitability at Gillette and printer cartridges to the profitability of HP. Razor blades and printer cartridges, respectively, are the golden nuggets at these companies, the primary drivers of profits. What are the golden nuggets at your company? What about the golden nuggets of your competitors or your industry overall? You need to know what your golden nuggets are to choose investments that will provide your stakeholders with the highest possible returns. You should concentrate your investments in areas that will drive your golden nuggets to create value.

The Roadmap's assessment of business impact in Chapter 4 provides the tools to determine your company's golden nuggets now and in the future. It's critical that you take the time to determine the key operational levers that drive revenue, margins, and ultimately higher cash flows for your company. You must know your company's golden nuggets to use the Roadmap today and to create strategies for future growth.

Risk Analysis

Risk is pervasive and underlies the entire process of evaluating and executing investments. You should think about risk from start to finish every time you undertake or even consider making an investment. Does your company consider risk using a disciplined approach like the one the Roadmap describes in Chapter 5? What risk mitigation strategies do you use in the investment process?

Risk and how you deal with it can mean the difference between bridging the execution gap and falling into the valley of failure. The Roadmap helps you develop methodologies you can use to assess and mitigate risk for your investments. Some investments might promise high returns but be too risky to warrant corporate resources. On the other hand, too many companies seek to minimize all risk in all situations, and, as a result, they do not make the investments they need to provide high returns to shareholders.

As you evaluate investments, remember that one of the most important components of risk analysis is to consider individual investments as options within portfolios of investments whenever possible. A one-shot investment such as a computer software package cannot be treated like a portfolio option; you can only invest in one system, and the system you install has to work. Instead of having a relatively small number of investments that require a significant commitment of resources, many companies have found that it is better to have a large number of investments that require a lower commitment of resources. As progress is made, uncertainty is resolved, and you can then decide which investments to continue and which to terminate.

Execution

The foundation of the Business Investment Roadmap is execution. Recalling some of the examples cited in Chapter 6 of investments that failed because of execution problems, can some of the difficulties your company has experienced be explained by problems in execution? Execution analysis is determining the who, what, when, where, why, and how of an investment. For your future investments, you must drill down as deeply as possible to obtain the details of the who, what, when, where, why, and how in order to feel confident that your investment will succeed. This process is the essence of the Business Investment Roadmap.

Execution is the critical switching point from ideas and talk to reality and results. Make sure that the proponents of an investment recognize that the "devil is in the details" and provide you with the information that you need to evaluate their proposed investment thoroughly. It is lack of attention to those details that often cause the failure of investments.

The Roadmap includes tools to evaluate the impact of investments on customers and prospects. Customers are the reason why companies exist, and you must consider the impact on your customers and your prospects when evaluating investments. Similarly, execution requires you to consider the capital intensity of investments. The Roadmap also includes a tool called "How many Yeses?" for assessing the complexity of an investment and the difficulty of making an investment successful. This simple question can guide your company toward successful investments and away from failures, across a whole spectrum of investments–new products or services, acquisitions, R&D, and HRM initiatives.

Ongoing Management

Do you remember the Fleetwood Mac song "Don't Stop Thinking About Tomorrow?" That phrase applies to ongoing management, but it only tells part of the story. You can't just think about tomorrow, you need to anticipate situations and take action depending on what happens tomorrow with your investments.

Ongoing management is extremely important to the success of your investment, but strangely it is often ignored. Somehow, managers forget to think about tomorrow after their investments are made today. Don't let this happen to you. Think about investments you have been involved with in the past. Did your team pay sufficient attention to ongoing management issues?

It is usually a very long and arduous journey from the time that a resource commitment is made to success and growth in corporate value. An important part of your job in applying the Roadmap is to develop and apply metrics to evaluate performance of your investments from start to finish. Unfortunately, developing the proper metrics to measure investment performance can be difficult. Everyone knows that it is important to have metrics for time and budgets, but it is just as critical, and often overlooked, to have metrics that track what is being delivered.

The Roadmap tools in Chapter 7 will help you to stay on course with your investments. One approach, EVA, has been used successfully by a wide range of organizations, including the U.S. Department of Defense, major corporations, and startup ventures. Although it can be an effective approach, you do not have to adopt EVA to stay on course; what is important is that you have a disciplined and consistent approach for monitoring the status of your investments. The information you get from an approach customized to your needs will enable you to make the inevitable changes in your execution plans as circumstances change. At times, these changes will lead you to the conclusion that your company should not continue to provide resources to specific investments and, instead, exercise options to pursue other investments that have been more successful at reaching milestones.

Building the Bridge Between Strategy and Finance

The Business Investment Roadmap is the bridge between strategy and finance. It is not a substitute for either strategy or finance, but it is an important and critical complement that enables you to evaluate and execute investments to grow corporate value.

The Business Investment Roadmap will help your company to make smarter and better investment choices. However, it is important to keep in mind that there are no miracle cures or simple and easy solutions to ensure corporate or personal success. There is no panacea that will work for every company in every situation. Just the opposite often holds true. What works for one company in one industry at a particular time might not necessarily work for that same company in the future or for another company at any point in time. The best you can do is to develop and use a disciplined and consistent methodology that is flexible enough to change with the needs of your company.

With the Roadmap in hand, you are ready to begin to apply it at your company. As your first step on the road to successful investments, review the "Following the Roadmap" sections in Chapters 3 through 7, where you will find more detailed explanations and examples of how to put the Business Investment Roadmap into action. These examples can serve as templates with the work you do evaluating and executing investments. Applying the Business Investment Roadmap requires some familiarity with accounting and finance, so you can refer to the Appendix if you want a quick refresher.

Because it is founded on business basics, the Business Investment Roadmap becomes almost automatic after awhile. Best of all, like Indiana Jones in *Indiana Jones and The Last Crusade,* when evaluating investments, you will be able to "choose wisely."

A

ACCOUNTING AND FINANCE: SOME BACKGROUND ON TOOLS OF THE TRADE

There's no business like show business,
but there are several businesses like accounting.

David Letterman

At this point, you have read the book and are ready to put the Business Investment Roadmap to use in making investments at your company. Although you do not need a background in accounting and finance to use the Business Investment Roadmap, you do need to get certain information from your company's financial statements. With this in mind, this Appendix is meant to give you an overview of financial statements and their component parts. It focuses on the elements that are most affected by investments and how these effects translate into cash flows and shareholder value creation. We use Fresh Breeze, the same composite company we used in the "Following the Roadmap" sections of the book, as the example in the Appendix, but you should read the Appendix with your own company's financial statements handy for reference.

Before we work our way through the financial statements, we should note that if you look at the numbers in any financial statement in isolation, they usually won't tell you very much. You need to consider them in terms of the company's historical financial performance and the financial performance of other companies in the industry. In other words, you need comparison ratios to evaluate the performance of your company against its past performance and against other companies in the industry. The Appendix explains and illustrates situations in which you should make a few simple calculations to make the numbers in the financial statements easier.

Income Statement

The income statement summarizes the results of operations over a period of time: revenues, costs, and income. The income statement is one of the easiest and most obvious ways to gauge performance: At the most basic level, sales minus costs equals income. Common-size financial statements are financial statements expressed as percentages; income statement items are expressed as a percentage of sales. Common-size financial statements allow us either to compare different companies directly or to look at the performance of a single company over time. Table A.1 shows the consolidated income statements and common-size income statements for Fresh Breeze from year 2000 through 2002.

Table A.1 Fresh Breeze Corporation Income and Common-Size Income Statements, 2000–2002

($Millions)	Income Statement			Common-Size		
	2000	2001	2002	2000	2001	2002
Sales	$1,000	$1,050	$1,103	100%	100%	100%
Less Total Cost of Goods Sold	$437	$459	$482	43.7%	43.7%	43.7%
Gross Margin	$563	$591	$620	56.3%	56.3%	56.2%
Less SG&A Expenses	$350	$367	$386	35.0%	35.0%	35.0%
Less Depreciation	$45	$50	$55	4.5%	4.8%	5.0%
Earnings before interest and taxes (EBIT)	$168	$173	$179	16.8%	16.5%	16.2%
Less Interest Expense	$22	$22	$22	2.2%	2.1%	2.0%
Pre-Tax Income	$146	$151	$157	14.6%	14.4%	14.2%
Less Taxes	$51	$53	$55	5.1%	5.0%	5.0%
Net Income	$95	$98	$102	9.5%	9.3%	9.2%
Dividends Paid to Shareholders	$10	$10	$10	1.0%	1.0%	0.9%
Retained Earnings	$85	$88	$92	8.5%	8.4%	8.3%

Sales

Sales usually means revenue, returns, and allowances. Fresh Breeze's sales figures allow us to calculate a critical ratio, the sales growth rate, as shown in Table A.2. Sales at Fresh Breeze have been growing at 5 percent per year for the last several years. This is steady, if relatively slow growth, typical for a well-established consumer products company like Fresh Breeze.

Knowing your company's sales growth rate is essential to the investment decision-making process; it serves as a baseline and a reality check. If your company has grown at 1 percent per year for the past five years, it might not be able to absorb an investment expected to double revenues every two years, even if you have estimated the value of the investment accurately. In addition, increasing the sales growth rate is the most effective way to increase

Table A.2 Fresh Breeze Corporation Sales Growth Rate and Expected Sales Growth Rate, 2001–2007

($Millions)	2001	2002	2003	2004	2005	2006	2007
Sales	$1,050	$1,103	$1,158	$1,216	$1,277	$1,340	$1,408
Sales Growth	$50	$53	$55	$58	$61	$63	$68
Sales Growth Rate	5%	5%	5%	5%	5%	5%	5%

profitability. Doing so requires an increase in working capital to finance and to supply the increase in sales.

Cost of Goods Sold (COGS)

Cost of Good Sold (COGS) includes all of the costs directly incurred in the production of a company's products. For Fresh Breeze, this includes raw materials, utilities, and wage expenses of production personnel, as well as other costs directly related to production. In 2001, Fresh Breeze's COGS was $459 million; COGS increased to $482 million in 2001. This doesn't mean much on its own; after all, sales are growing, so we should expect COGS to grow as well. What is more important to note is that COGS remained steady at 43.7 percent as a percentage of sales, which means that Fresh Breeze is neither gaining any cost efficiencies or economies of scale nor becoming less efficient at producing goods as its sales grow.

Gross Margin (GM)

Gross Margin (GM) is sales minus COGS, which for Fresh Breeze was $620 million in 2002. GM measures profitability, and it compares the cost of the goods or services provided to the prices obtained for selling them. As we would expect, because COGS has remained constant, GM has remained constant as well. If GM were to decline over time, it would be a strong danger signal to management.

You will often find it useful to track GM percentages. Higher COGS percentages result in lower GM percentages. Lower GMs might be due to the costs of raw materials going up, the company becoming less efficient, average revenue per product sold declining, or some other factor. A few percentage points of margin can make a big difference in many industries. For example, in the shoe manufacturing business, companies have found that it is much cheaper to make shoes in countries with low wage rates, even factoring in the higher costs of shipping and other costs of manufacturing.

Sales, General, and Administrative (SG&A) Expenses include selling and marketing expenses, expenses associated with headquarters and other nonproduction facilities, and other costs and expenses not directly associated with production. Fresh Breeze's SG&A expenses have grown in absolute terms, but more important, they have remained at a constant 35 percent of sales. This is a possible area of concern for the company, because it should achieve some efficiency in its SG&A expenses as revenues grow.

Depreciation Expense

Depreciation expense is the portion of the costs of capital assets being converted to expenses during the period. For Fresh Breeze, depreciation reflects the cost amortization of the company's property, plant, equipment, and other long-term assets. The company had depreciation expenses of $45 million, $50 million, and $55 million in 2000, 2001, and 2002, respectively. Depreciation is not a cash expense; thus, an increase in year-to-year depreciation or an increase in depreciation as a percentage of revenues should not cause the same level of concern as other expenses.

In theory, the depreciation expense deduction should provide a company with a way to expense an investment in a fixed asset gradually over time. Assume that a company buys a piece of equipment for $900 and that the equipment has a "useful life" of three years. The useful life is set by the Internal Revenue Service (IRS); it might not reflect the actual life of the asset. Using straight-line depreciation (divide the amount paid for the asset by its useful life), the company would deduct $300 per year as a depreciation expense. As we noted earlier, this expense is not a cash outlay of

$300. The cash associated with purchasing this asset is recorded at the time of sale if it was a cash purchase. If it was purchased on credit, it is recorded as the company pays off its financing terms. The $300 depreciation represents the amount that the company is allowed to subtract from its income to reflect the decline in value of the piece of equipment. With this $300 depreciation, effectively the company can shield $300 in cash income from being taxed (depreciation is taken out before taxes are calculated).

In reality, depreciation often works quite differently from theory. In the given example, assume that the IRS decides to change the useful life of the piece of equipment from three years to two years. The company could then deduct $450 ($900 divided by two years) for two years, rather than $300 for three years. The company's taxable income will be less in those years. The faster depreciation rate clearly benefits both the asset buyer, who can more rapidly shield more of its income up front, and the manufacturer and seller of the equipment, because the effective increase in return to the buyer makes the purchase more attractive. This is why equipment manufacturers often seek to have the government shorten depreciation schedules.

Depreciation schedules rarely are accurate, particularly if you consider obsolescence rather than functional life. Think about the perfectly functioning electronic items—cell phones, personal organizers, TVs, PCs, and CD players—that get abandoned because newer models have new features that we want. A computer with a useful life of three years according to the IRS might have a much shorter actual life because of obsolescence.

Earnings Before Interest and Taxes (EBIT)

Earnings Before Interest and Taxes (EBIT), another profitability measure, is GM minus SG&A expenses and depreciation. Although Fresh Breeze's EBIT has increased in absolute terms, it has decreased as a percentage of sales, largely due to the increase in depreciation expense. Because this drop is due to depreciation expenses rather than operating issues, it is not a major concern of management.

Interest Expense

Interest expense is the interest a company pays on its debt; for Fresh Breeze, interest expense remained constant at $22 million from 2000 through 2002. The company has not taken on any new net debt over the last few years. Depending on the type of investment under consideration, and whether you plan to finance it with debt or equity, interest expense might be an important factor in estimating the profitability of your investment.

Pretax Income

Pretax income is another profitability measure; it is the difference between EBIT and interest expense, sometimes referred to as earnings before taxes (EBT). Pretax income is important because it is the earnings number to which the tax rate is applied to determine taxes. Fresh Breeze had $146 million in pretax income in 2000, which rose to $151 million in 2001, and $157 million in 2002. As a percentage of sales, pretax income has fallen only slightly over the past few years.

Taxes

Taxes are calculated by multiplying pretax earnings by the tax rate. Fresh Breeze's taxes have increased in proportion to its pretax income. Note that the tax amounts that appear in the income statement often are different from the actual taxes paid. The reasons for this difference are well beyond our scope here, but the difference stems from the fact that in the United States, tax policies and accounting rules are determined independently. The government determines tax policy, and accounting standards are formulated by a private organization, the Financial Accounting Standards Board (FASB).

Net Income

Net income is the most basic and most important profitability measure, calculated as pretax income minus taxes. More broadly, net income is a company's earnings after all costs and expenses have been subtracted. Fresh Breeze's net income rose from $95 million in 2000, to $98 million in 2001, and $102 million in 2002. Managers and investors should be extremely alert to changes in net income, as it is often the profitability measure most examined by markets and investors. A related and equally important number is earnings per share (EPS), calculated by taking net income and dividing it by the number of shares a company has outstanding. These are the figures most commonly cited to indicate company performance. Analysts devote an inordinate amount of time predicting EPS down to the penny, and companies manipulate their financial statements to meet investor and Wall Street earnings expectations.

Dividends Paid to Shareholders

Net income is either distributed to shareholders in the form of dividends or kept within the company to finance growth. A company's board of directors generally sets dividend policy. Fresh Breeze paid out $10 million in dividends each year from 2000 through 2002. Because dividends remained steady even as net income rose, the proportion of earnings distributed to shareholders has been decreasing. Fresh Breeze might need to reconsider its dividend policy and offer larger dividends to its shareholders, or more effectively invest its earnings to provide future returns.

Retained Earnings

Retained earnings is the portion of net income that is not distributed to shareholders as dividends but, rather, is retained by the company to fuel future growth. Fresh Breeze's retained earnings rose from $85 million in 2000 to $92 million in 2002. The company should either find more effective ways to invest its earnings to provide future returns to shareholders or give more of its earnings back to shareholders as dividends.

Balance Sheet

The balance sheet is a snapshot view of a company's assets, liabilities, and equities at a point in time; it consists of the following elements:

- Assets: The items of economic value that the company owns.

- Liabilities: The financial obligations or debts that the company owes against its assets.

- Equity: The ownership interest in the corporation in the form of stock.

Assets are Equal to Liabilities Plus Equities.

On the balance sheet, both assets and liabilities are presented in order of liquidity (how close they are to being converted to cash). Current assets and current liabilities are expected to be converted to cash (assets) or paid in cash (liabilities) during the next year. Table A.3 contains the balance sheet and common-size balance sheet for Fresh Breeze, Inc. for 1999 through 2002. They describe the assets, liabilities, and equities of the company on December 31 of each year. As with the income statement, on its own, the balance

Table A.3   Fresh Breeze Corporation Balance Sheets and Common-Size Balance Sheets, Year-End December 31, 1999–2002

Year	1999	2000	2001	2002	1999	2000	2001	2002
($Millions)								
Assets								
Cash	$35	$86	$141	$216	5.6%	12.0%	17.5%	23.7%
Inventory	$44	$45	$47	$49	7.0%	6.3%	5.8%	5.4%
Accounts Receivable	$150	$154	$161	$170	23.8%	21.6%	20.0%	18.7%
Total Current Assets	$229	$284	$350	$435	36.4%	39.8%	43.5%	47.8%
Gross Property, Plant & Equipment	$400	$475	$550	$625				
Less Accumulated Depreciation	$0	-$45	-$95	-$150				
Net Property, Plant & Equipment	$400	$430	$455	$475	63.6%	60.2%	56.5%	52.2%
Total Assets	**$629**	**$714**	**$805**	**$910**	100%	100%	100%	100%
Liabilities and Shareholder Equity								
Liabilities								
Accounts Payable	$44	$45	$47	$49	7.0%	6.3%	5.8%	5.4%
Bank Notes Payable	$35	$35	$35	$35	5.6%	4.9%	4.3%	3.9%
Total Current Liabilities	$79	$80	$82	$84	12.6%	11.2%	10.2%	9.3%
Long-Term Debt	$250	$250	$250	$250	39.7%	35.0%	31.1%	27.8%
Total Liabilities	*$329*	*$330*	*$332*	*$334*	52.3%	46.2%	41.2%	37.1%
Equity								
Shareholders Equity	$300	$300	$300	$300	47.7%	42.0%	37.3%	33.3%
Retained Earnings	$0	$85	$173	$265	0.0%	11.9%	21.5%	29.4%
Total Equity	*$300*	*$385*	*$473*	*$565*	47.7%	53.9%	58.8%	62.8%
Total Liabilities and Equity	**$629**	**$714**	**$805**	**$900**	100%	100%	100%	100%

sheet is of limited use. The common-size balance sheet, which shows items as a percentage of total assets, is included with the balance sheet to provide more information.

Assets

Assets are the economic resources that a company has at the point in time that the balance sheet was made. Assets are typically listed in order of liquidity, from most to least liquid.

Cash: Cash usually means cash and cash equivalents (marketable securities, etc.); companies typically do not keep a large proportion of their liquid assets around as cash because they can earn a return on them by investing in liquid financial instruments such as money market funds and marketable securities (like certificates of deposit). Fresh Breeze's cash position has improved significantly, from $86 million at the end of 2000 to $216 million in 2002. More importantly, cash as a percentage of assets has also increased, from 12 percent in 2000, to 23.7 percent in 2002. Although generating cash is definitely a good thing, the increase in the cash percentage of assets suggests that the company might not be managing its cash reserves and working capital for optimum growth. Depending on the company's investment plans, it probably has too much cash on its hands. However, sometimes having too much cash is the best option available. Microsoft has incredible cash reserves, in part because the company does not believe it can get a sufficient return by investing all of its cash in its own operations.

Inventory: Inventory refers to raw materials, work in progress, and finished inventory that a company has not yet sold. Fresh Breeze's inventory levels have increased in absolute terms but have fallen from 6.3 percent of assets to 5.4 percent of assets. Although low inventory levels are generally a good thing, Fresh Breeze might have depleted its inventory too much; it might be in danger of not being able to service its accounts adequately.

A different, and in many ways better performance ratio, inventory as a percentage of COGS, shows that inventory seems to be growing at a rate consistent with the growth of COGS. Fresh Breeze's inventory as a percentage of COGS has remained steady at 10 percent over the last couple of years, as shown in Table A.4.

Table A.4   Fresh Breeze Corporation Inventory as a Percentage of COGS, 2001–2002

	2000	2001	2002
COGS ($ Million)		$459	$482
Inventory, Year-End ($ Million)	$45	$47	$49
Average Inventory ($ Million)		$46	$48
Aveage Inventory as a Percentage of COGS		**10%**	**10%**

A quick comment on this calculation: COGS is from the income statement and represents the costs for the entire year, whereas inventory from the balance sheet is inventory at a specific date; thus, you should take the average of the inventory at the beginning and at the end of the year. Remember that the end of one year (December 31) is equivalent to the beginning of the next year (January 1).

Accounts Receivable: Accounts Receivable (A/R) are sales that a company has made to customers on credit. It represents uncollected revenues. Receivables at Fresh Breeze have increased in absolute terms, but they have dropped as a percentage of assets from 21.6 percent in 2000 to 18.7 percent in 2002. Customers are paying Fresh Breeze faster than they have in past years. This is a trend that the company would like to see continue; the faster customers pay for goods, the lower the carrying cost of receivables, and the more profitable sales become. On the other hand, if accounts receivable were drifting upwards as a percentage of sales, it might be cause for concern at the company. When customers are slow to pay their bills, a company is forced to finance accounts receivable. The financing costs the company money. Think of a situation where your employer didn't pay you for several months; you would need to arrange financing from a bank or another source to pay your own bills.

Total Current Assets: Total current assets are the sum of cash, inventory, and accounts receivable. Because its component parts have increased, it is not surprising that total current assets at Fresh Breeze have increased as well. The total current assets subtotal is useful in looking at the company's liquidity. Company management of current assets can also be a key driver of business success, particularly in the retail and distribution industries.

It is often said that "retail is detail." This statement reflects the importance of knowing what customers will buy and making sure that there is sufficient, but not excessive, inventory for meeting the demand. Many retailers have failed by managing their inventories poorly. In the past few years, for example, Gap Corporation, owner of the Gap, Old Navy, and Banana Republic stores, has had difficulty with its merchandise mix. The company has experienced declining sales and increasing inventory, which has to be marked down. These markdowns in turn erode profit margins.

Current asset management is also critical to the success of manufacturers. Dell Computer, one of the great success stories of the past decade, has used current asset management to create a strategic advantage over other PC manufacturers like HP. Think about this for a moment: Dell gets customers to pay for the product before it is made and shipped. It receives money from customers up front, while waiting at least 30 days to pay its suppliers. By contrast, HP ships to retailers and waits to get paid. Which company is doing a better job managing its cash conversion cycle?

Dell is in a much stronger financial position than HP. Instead of financing the costs of inventory and accounts receivable, it has very little to finance. In fact, Dell has *your* money to invest during the float on the money it owes suppliers. Compared with industry averages, this working capital management was worth more than $100 million to Dell in fiscal 2001.

Long-Term Assets and Accumulated Depreciation: Long-term assets, such as property, plant, and equipment, reflect prior investment decisions by the company. These are the assets that you can see. To some people, they are a reflection of the strength and sustainability of a company. During the past several years, some observers have suggested that long-term assets should be minimized because of the high capital investment required, the obsolescence risk, and the low return on investment. This thinking has been an important factor behind many companies' moves toward outsourcing, particularly to offshore locations.

Sometimes it does not make sense to invest in fixed assets. Factories and equipment decay, and the waste is senseless when the assets were designed to make a product that is no longer in demand. There is not much that a company can do with these devalued assets, and in fast-moving markets, it often does not make sense to invest in fixed assets to handle all of your needs. Indeed, as we discussed in an earlier chapter, several of the financial metrics used to evaluate performance are based on how well the company is using its assets. Producing the same level of revenues and margins with fewer fixed assets is clearly superior to producing the same revenues with greater amounts of fixed assets. In the first case, management is effectively providing greater returns to shareholders at a lower investment.

On the other hand, this view can go too far. Consider Enron, which actively sought to divest itself of its fixed assets because management felt it could get higher returns on trading and related activities. Ironically, the only value Enron had after its downfall was in fixed assets like pipelines. Of course, Enron is an extreme example, but many managers feel that it is better to invest wisely in fixed plant and equipment because of risks associated with outsourcing critical processes.

Depreciation: Depreciation is the accounting convention that allows companies to convert capital costs to expenses over time. As we saw from the income statement in Table A.1, depreciation reduces net income without any effect on cash flow. Because taxes are calculated from net income, not cash flow, depreciation allows companies to make tax deductions out of their capital investments. Keep in mind, however, that fixed assets are recorded at their book value on the balance sheet and that the market value of those assets is likely to be quite different.

Let's take a look at the Fresh Breeze balance sheet (Table A.3) to get more perspective on fixed assets. The company's only important long-term assets are its property, plant, and equipment. As of 2000, the company had gross property, plant, and equipment of $475 million, and it made capital expenditures of $75 million each in 2001 and 2002. Accumulated depreciation is the total amount of depreciation to date on Fresh Breeze's long-term assets.

Intangible Assets: Intangible assets encompass essentially all nonphysical assets, typically related to customers, technology, marketing, and goodwill. Businesses invest constantly to acquire and to build intangible assets. The value of a company's intangible assets can and often does exceed the value of the assets shown on the balance sheet. As of the end of fiscal 2002, Coca-Cola's market capitalization (the value of the company based on its stock price multiplied by the number of shares outstanding) was much higher than its fixed assets. The difference between the two reflects the value of the company's intangible assets, including its "secret formula" for Coke, brand name, know-how, and distribution channels. In fact, it is the other intangible assets besides the formula that create most of the value. If you were given the formula for Coke today, but you couldn't sell it under the Coke brand or promote it as the same as Coke, it would not have much value to you.

Nearly every company has intangible assets, and for some companies, those assets have significant value. Compare Microsoft, which does not have much in the way of fixed assets (no factories, not much equipment), with Ford, which has many factories and high investment in equipment. Many of those intangible assets at

Microsoft, however, like those at Enron, leave on the elevator every night with the employees.

Although we did not include them as a separate line item, Fresh Breeze likely has many intangible assets, including the brand names of the company's products; the company's know-how in developing, manufacturing, and distributing products; and intellectual property, such as copyrights and patents. These intangible assets would not show up on the balance sheet unless they were either purchased or somehow acquired from another source. Intangible assets that are developed within a company show up intrinsically as increases in market capitalization.

Total Assets: The total assets are the sum of current and fixed assets.

Liabilities

Liabilities are the financial obligations of a company; together with equity, they are often thought of as the source of funds for the assets listed in the top half of the balance sheet. Like assets, liabilities are listed in order of liquidity (when they are due to be paid in cash).

Accounts Payable (A/P): A/P is the amount that a company owes to suppliers or other vendors for products or services the company has purchased on credit. In the context of the cash conversion cycle, A/P has the opposite effect on cash from accounts receivable. The longer a company takes to cover its payables with cash (within the time allowed by its vendors), the better its cash position, and the more opportunity it has to take advantage of the float (recall the Dell Computer example). Although Fresh Breeze's payables have increased in absolute terms over the last few years, they have decreased as a percentage of assets. The faster a company clears its payables, the less it is forcing its suppliers to finance its purchases. Fresh Breeze might be paying its receivables too quickly.

Notes Payable: Notes payable are short-term bank notes or commercial paper that must be repaid within the year. There are a wide variety of types of debt; many balance sheets also show lines for current portion of long-term debt, or other debt instruments with current payments due. Fresh Breeze's notes payable have remained constant in absolute terms over the last three years, but they have decreased as a percentage as the company's assets have grown.

Total Current Liabilities: Total current liabilities, the sum of accounts payable, bank notes payable, and other current liabilities, is often useful in looking at a company's liquidity and evaluating its ability to meet its short-term obligations. Fresh Breeze's total current liabilities increased only slightly, and they have decreased relative to total assets.

Long-Term Debt: Long-term debt is like your home mortgage; it represents past borrowings by a company in the form of loans, bonds, and other debt instruments. Fresh Breeze has had $250 million in bonds on its books for the last three years.

Total Liabilities: Fresh Breeze's total liabilities have increased only slightly. Total liabilities as a percentage of total assets is a variation on an important ratio, debt:equity. Fresh Breeze has lowered its debt percentage considerably, from 46.2 percent of assets in 2000 to 37.1 percent of assets in 2002. This shift is a result of the company's large retained earnings over the last three years.

Equity

Shareholders' Equity: Shareholders' equity is often divided between the par value of the stock issued (usually a nominal value per share, such as $0.01) and additional paid-in capital, which is the amount over the par value investors paid for the stock. Remember that shareholders' equity on the balance sheet does not represent the market value of the stock shares; the balance sheet is merely capturing the investment that was made in the company. Fresh Breeze has shareholders' equity of $300 million, which means that the company raised $300 million when it issued shares in the company.

Retained Earnings: Fresh Breeze's 2000 retained earnings of $85 million mean that cumulatively, the company had retained $85 million of its net income within the business. Retained earnings grew by net income minus dividends paid in each year, reaching $265 million at the end of 2002. It is important to keep two things in mind:

- Liabilities plus equities must equal assets.

- Retained earnings are not equivalent to cash.

Total Equity: Total equity is the amount that investors or owners put into the company in exchange for stock shares (shareholders' equity), as well as income created by and retained by the company (retained earnings). For publicly traded companies, the shares outstanding are part of the equity shown.

Total Liabilities and Equity: Total liabilities and equity should equal total assets, a relationship that provides a quick way to check for consistency in a balance sheet. The impact on the balance sheet of investments that increase sales or reduce costs depends on the specifics of the investment, but they can affect nearly every area of the balance sheet. The important changes are the ones that affect cash flow, as we shall see in the next section.

Statement of Cash Flows

The statement of cash flows takes information from the balance sheet and income statement to describe the cash inflows and outflows during the reporting period. Cash flows are divided into operating, investing, and financing activities. The key here is that the cash flow statement starts out with net income and adjusts it by all of the cash inflows and outflows to arrive at a net cash flow.

Why is this necessary? Take depreciation as an example. Depreciation is subtracted from sales in the calculation of net income. It is not a cash transaction; it is not a transaction at all, but an accounting mechanism to allow companies to amortize capital expenses over time. Depreciation does not affect real cash income; thus, it is added back to net income in the operating activities section.

Operating activities include net income and the adjustments you must make to net income because it is accrual income and not cash income. Investing activities include buying and selling capital assets and investments in other securities that are not cash equivalents. Financing activities include issuing and retiring new debt and stock issues, as well as dividend payments. Figure A.1 shows the adjustments that you commonly must make to calculate cash flows from your balance sheet and income statement.

Why do you add a decrease in accounts receivable and subtract an increase? Accounts receivable are the sums that someone else owes you for sales that have been made on credit; they are not cash on hand. Because the customer has not yet paid for the sales,

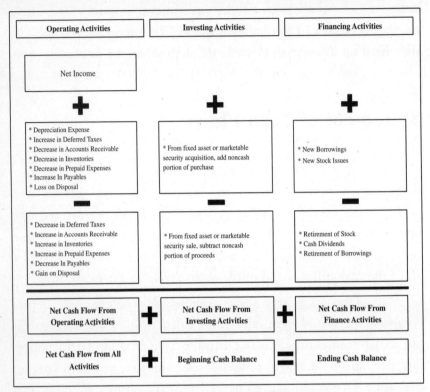

Figure A.1   Flowchart for Calculating Free Cash Flows

accounts receivable count as income, but it is not cash income. If accounts receivable increases over the course of a year, it means that more sales are tied up in receivables, and less cash is available at a given level of sales. Likewise, a decrease in accounts receivable means that more customers have paid, and the company has received additional cash.

Sales and Accounts Receivable

We noted earlier that the financial statements are all related. At this point, it is important to discuss one of the most important relationships, sales and accounts receivable. As we discussed earlier, a company's sales are tracked on the income statement at the top line. Sales are the lifeblood of the business, and growth in sales is often used as a metric for the success of a company. This was particularly true during the late 1990s, when many companies and investors subscribed to the notion that revenue growth was more important than profitability.

Nearly every company wants to grow revenues, but what happens after the sale is made? If the sale is for cash, the company gets the cash, and it shows up on the balance sheet as cash. A more typical situation, however, is for the company to provide financing to the customer. The customer buys the products or services (revenue) and then has a period of time to pay, for example, 30 days. From the perspective of the company making the sale, although the revenue shows up on the income statement, it has yet to be collected (become cash), creating accounts receivable.

If you are a salesperson who gets paid a commission based on sales, you do your best to maximize sales. However, there is a major difference between making the sale and getting the cash. Your company has to track the accounts receivable and collect it from the buyer. If the buyer won't pay or has sufficient market leverage over you (e.g., if the products you sell are readily available somewhere else, buyers don't need to worry about being cut off by you), your company cannot collect. Unless your company can collect its receivables, it will rapidly be out of business. Even if you receive your sales commissions, you will soon be out of a job.

This example might oversimplify things, but it points out a significant relationship between the sales revenue on the income statement and accounts receivable on the balance sheet. Many managers and companies have played a game of showing increased revenues when, in fact, the revenues come from sales to customers that were either very poor credit risks or simply did not pay. Consider, for example, the boom in sales of telecommunications equipment during the late 1990s. Many of the customers were small companies just getting into the business (called competitive local exchange carriers) or Internet service providers that were never going to be able to grow their businesses and profits fast enough to pay for the equipment. The major telecommunications equipment providers ignored the credit risk and made the sales anyway, and now they suffer the consequence of having to write off massive amounts of their receivables. Lucent at one time had more than $7 billion in outstanding accounts receivable, and now a good portion of this money will likely never be collected. Lucent should never have extended credit terms to many of those customers.

By now, you should see the need to recognize the relationship between sales and accounts receivable. At the most basic level, most companies need more capital as their sales increase, because their receivables will increase. We call this an increase in working capital, because most companies need to grow current assets as revenues grow, even if they are turning their inventory and receivables at the same or even faster rates.

There are also many examples of corporate mischief with revenue and accounts receivable. Recently, for example, Gillette acknowledged that it had grown sales by what is commonly called "stuffing the channel." The company's products had been pushed to wholesalers and retailers at a rate that far surpassed the rate they could sell to their customers. Temporarily, the growth was great for Gillette, but the day of reckoning came suddenly when new orders for products declined precipitously because retailers already had excess inventory. In the equity markets, Gillette's stock price fell by many dollars when the company announced and adjusted for this problem. As expected, many of the senior managers at Gillette have since left the company.

Although the actions of Gillette's management were wrong, they were not illegal. There have been several such cases of corporate wrongdoing driven by a desire to show increased revenue while ignoring the impact on receivables. Several years ago, management at a manufacturer of computer equipment decided to show revenue growth by shipping boxes filled with bricks. The revenue numbers showed growth and although the accounts receivable were, of course, never going to be collected, management was able to keep the stock price higher than it otherwise would have been, at least until the fraud became apparent. More recently, several of the dot-com companies have acknowledged that they engaged in transactions that boosted revenue while creating receivables that were not likely to be collected. Many of these companies have since gone bankrupt.

Adjustments

Turning back to our exhibit, not all of the adjustments work in the same direction. For example, an increase in accounts payable is added to net income because the cash the company will use to pay the account has not yet been spent and is still in the company's possession.

Table A.5 shows Fresh Breeze's statement of cash flows for 2000 through 2002, and the elements of the cash flow statement (with their source in parentheses) are as follows:

Cash provided (used) by operating activities

- Net income, the first entry in the operating activities section, was $102 million in 2002 (2002 income statement).

- Depreciation of $55 million is added back to net income (2002 income statement) because depreciation is not a cash expense.

- Inventory increased $2 million, from $47 million at the end of 2001 to $49 million at the end of 2002 (2001 and 2002 balance sheet). Because creating inventory requires cash, increasing inventory must be subtracted from operating activities. In contrast, if inventories had gone down, the difference would be added to cash flow, because inventory had been squeezed out into additional sales.

- Accounts receivable increased by $9 million, from $161 million in 2001 to $170 million in 2002 (2001 and 2002 balance sheet). Although accounts receivable count as income in the income statement, and we can assume the company will eventually be paid, they are sales that have been made but not yet paid for by customers. The increase in accounts receivable, therefore, must be subtracted out of operating cash flows. Conversely, a decrease in accounts receivable is added to operating cash flows because customers have paid for more of their purchases with cash.

- Accounts payable increased by $2 million, from $47 million in 2000 to $49 million in 2002 (2001 and 2002 balance sheets). An increase in accounts payable must be added to operating cash flows because it means the company is making additional purchases that it has not yet paid for—it still has the cash in hand. Decreasing accounts payable must be subtracted from operating cash flows because it means that the company is paying its bills faster (so it has less cash on hand).

- The sum of net income and these adjustments is $139 million, meaning that Fresh Breeze created $139 million in cash from operating activities in 2002.

Cash provided (used) by investing activities

- From a review of the financials for 2001 and 2002, Fresh Breeze had capital expenditures of $75 million in 2002, which it paid in cash. The net cash used by investing activities, therefore, was $75 million in 2002.

Cash provided (used) by financing activities

- Fresh Breeze paid $10 million in dividends to shareholders in 2002. This is a cash expense that is not factored into 2002 net income; thus, it is taken out as a cash cost of financing.

Net cash provided (used) by all activities, beginning, and ending cash

- Adding together net cash from operating, investing, and financing activities, Fresh Breeze generated $64 million in cash in 2002.

- Referring again to the balance sheets for 2001 and 2002, Fresh Breeze began 2002 with $141 million in cash and ended the year with $216 million in cash.

Table A.5   Fresh Breeze Corporation, Statements of Cash Flows, 2000–2002

Year	2000	2001	2002
($000s)			
Cash Provided (Used) by Operating Activities			
Net Income	$95	$98	$102
Plus Depreciation	$45	$50	$55
Change in Inventory (- Increase / +Decrease)	-$1	-$2	-$2
Change in Accounts Receivable (- Increase / + Decrease)	-$4	-$9	-$8
Change in Accounts Payable (+ Increase / - Decrease)	$1	$2	$2
Net Cash Provided (Used) by Operating Activities	**$136**	**$139**	**$149**
Cash Provided (Used) by Investing Activities			
Capital Expenditures	-$75	-$75	-$75
Net Cash Provided (Used) by Investing Activities	-$75	-$75	-$75
Cash Provided (Used) by Financing Activities			
Plus Net New Equity Capital Raised	$0	$0	$0
Less Dividends Paid	-$10	-$10	-$10
Plus Net New Long-term Debt	$0	$0	$0
Plus Net New Bank Borrowings	$0	$0	$0
Net Cash Provided (Used) by Financing Activities	**-$10**	**-$10**	**-$10**
Net Cash From All Activities	**$51**	**$54**	**$64**
Beginning Cash Balance	$35	$86	$141
Ending Cash Balance	$86	$141	$216

Financial Ratios and Other Ways to Spot Trends

A company's financial statements can tell you a great deal about its performance. However, numbers don't mean much in isolation; you need a way to look at the relationships among the numbers. Financial ratios can help, particularly when you compare ratios from a particular period with other periods for the company and, of course, with other companies in the industry. The commonly used terms *best practices* and *benchmarking* mean comparing the ratios from a given company to another that is an industry leader.

There are many financial ratios and combinations of financial ratios that you can use when analyzing financial statements. Some ratios have already been covered in our discussion of Fresh Breeze's financial statements, such as the sales growth rate, common-size financial statements, and the percentage of various income statement items of sales (COGS, GM, SG&A, EBIT, NI). There are many more, however, and several of them will be important tools in measuring and predicting the results of the investments your company makes.

Here are a few more major financial ratio categories (internal liquidity, operating performance, and liquidity) and how they would be calculated using Fresh Breeze's financials.

Internal Liquidity

Internal liquidity ratios compare current liabilities to current assets that will become available to meet those liabilities. There are two main types of internal liquidity ratios: ratios that directly compare current assets or a subset of current assets to current liabilities (current ratio, quick ratio, cash ratio) and ratios that measure the speed at which items on the balance sheet, such as receivables, inventory, and payables, turn over.

Fresh Breeze and the Cash Conversion Cycle

Fresh Breeze's current ratio improved from 2001 to 2002, as we can see in Table A.6. This appears to be a positive trend, but you should compare this to the industry or to competitors to see where the company really stands. Again, ratios should not be considered in isolation.

Fresh Breeze's receivables, inventory, and payables turnover rates have remained constant over the last three years. The company turns its receivables 6.7 times per year, its inventory 10 times per year, and its payables 10 times per year. Another way to look at these turnover rates is to look at the number of days it takes for receivables to be paid, for inventory to be processed and sold, and for Fresh Breeze to pay its own payables, by dividing 365 days by each turnover rate. We see that the days receivables outstanding remain at 54.8, the inventory processing period at 36.5, and the days payables remain at 36.5 days. The cash conversion cycle, the time it takes for the cash used to purchase raw materials to return through cash sales, is 54.8 days. To understand what these numbers mean in their entirety, we would need to compare them to numbers for other companies in the industry.

Table A.6   Fresh Breeze Corporation Internal Liquidity Ratios, 2001–2002

Ratio	Formula	2001	2002
Current Ratio	Current Assets / Current Liabilities	4.3	5.1
Receivables Turnover	Sales /Average Receivables	6.7	6.7
Days Receivables Outstanding (DRO)	365 / Receivables Turnover	54.8	54.8
Inventory Turnover	COGS / Average Inventory	10	10
Average Inventory Processing Period (AIPP)	365 / Inventory Turnover	36.5	36.5
Payables Turnover	COGS/ Average Payables	10	10
Payables Payment Period (PPP)	365 / Payables Turnover	36.5	36.5
Cash Conversion Cycle	DRO + AIPP - PPP	54.8	54.8

Operating Efficiency and Profitability Ratios

As their names suggest, operating efficiency and profitability ratios are ways to measure how efficient and profitable a company's operations are. The efficiency ratios (total asset turnover, net fixed asset turnover, and equity turnover) compare sales generated to assets or a subset of assets, in the form of sales per dollar of asset. A look at Fresh Breeze's operating efficiency ratios does not show much of a year-over-year change, except for net fixed asset turnover, the result of depreciation lowering the amount of net fixed assets. As Table A.7 illustrates, Fresh Breeze's margins have remained stable over the last three years.

Table A.7   Fresh Breeze Corporation Operating Efficiency and Profitability Ratios, 2001–2002

Ratio	Formula	2001	2002
Operating Efficiency			
Total Asset Turnover	Net Sales / Average Total Assets	1.4	1.3
Net Fixed Asset Turnover	Net Sales / Average Net Fixed Assets	2.4	2.4
Equity Turnover	Net Sales / Average Equity	2.4	2.1
Operating Profitability			
Gross Profit Margin	Gross Profit / Net Sales	0.6	0.6
Operating Profit Margin	Operating Profit / Net Sales	0.2	0.2
Net Profit Margin	Net Income / Net Sales	0.1	0.1
Return on Total Capital	(Net Income + Interest Expense) / Average Total Capital	0.2	0.1
Return on Equity	Net Income / Average Total Equity	0.2	0.2

Summary

Now that you have reviewed the major components of financial statements, you are ready to use your own company's financials as a tool for measuring the performance of the investments your company is currently involved in and for choosing better investments in the future. Financial statements are only the starting point on a long road of investment management, but starting with the solid financial basics will help you as you use the data you derive from financial statements to apply the Business Investment Roadmap to your company's investments.

BIBLIOGRAPHY

Alpert, Bill. "Now Hear This: Wall Street's Research Stinks. Here's How to Fix It," *Barron's*, December 2, 2002.

Axson, David. "Operational Risk Management: A New Performance Management Imperative," *Business Performance Management*, June 2003, pp. 34–40.

Bailey, Martin, N. "Information Technology and Productivity: Recent Findings," Presentation at the American Economic Association Annual Meetings, January 3, 2003.

Baker, Edward H., and Anne Field. "Project Management," *CIO Insight*, September 2001, pp. 57–67.

Baum, Geoff, et al. "Introducing a New Value Creation Index," *Forbes ASAP*, April 3, 2000.

Becker, Brian E., Mark A. Huselid, and Dave Ulrich. *The HR Scorecard: Linking People, Strategy, and Performance* (Boston: Harvard Business School Press, 2001).

Bernstein, Peter L. *Against the Gods: The Remarkable Story of Risk* (New York: John Wiley & Sons, 1998).

Blattberg, Robert C., Gary Getz, and Jacquelyn S. Thomas. *Customer Equity: Building and Managing Relationships as Valuable Assets* (Boston: Harvard Business School Press, 2001).

Bossidy, Larry, and Ram Charan. *Execution: The Discipline of Getting Things Done* (New York: Crown Business, 2002).

Collingwood, Harris, and Diane L. Coutu. "Jack on Jack: The HBR Interview," *Harvard Business Review*, February 2002, pp. 88–94.

Collins, Jim. *Good to Great: Why Some Companies Make the Leap and Others Don't* (New York: HarperBusiness, 2001).

Covey, Steven, A. Roger Merrill, and Rebecca R. Merrill *First Things First: To Live, to Love, to Learn, to Leave a Legacy* (New York: Simon & Schuster, 1994).

Dash, Julekha. "Training: Spending to Rise for Business, Security Risks," *Computerworld*, January 14, 2002, p. 30.

De Meyer, Arnoud, Christopher H. Loch, and Michael T. Pich. "Managing Project Uncertainty: From Variation to Chaos," *Sloan Management Review*, Winter 2002, pp. 60–67.

Drucker, Peter. "The Information Executives Truly Need," *Harvard Business Review*, January–February 1995.

Fama, Eugene F., and Kenneth R. French. "Industry Costs of Equity," *Journal of Financial Economics*, 43, 1997, pp. 153–193.

Farrell, Diana, Tara Terwilliger, and Alan P. Webb. "Getting IT Spending Right This Time," *The McKinsey Quarterly*, Second Quarter, 2003.

Gawande, Atul. *Complications* (New York: Metropolitan Books, 2002).

Gebhardt, William R., Charles M.C. Lee, and Bhaskaran Swaminathan. "Toward an Implied Cost of Capital," *Journal of Accounting Research*, Vol. 39, No. 1, June 2001, pp. 135–176.

Gompers, Paul A. "A Note on Valuation in Entrepreneurial Ventures," HBS Publishing, number 9-298-082, January 12, 1999.

Grove, Andrew S. *Only the Paranoid Survive: How to Exploit the Crisis Points That Challenge Every Company* (New York: Doubleday, 1999).

Hammer, Michael. "The Sufficient Company," *Harvard Business Review OnPoint*, Number 7699, 2000.

Harris, Trevor S., and Elmer H. Huh. "Valuing and Measuring a Technological Edge," *Global Valuation and Accounting Market Commentary/Strategy*, Morgan Stanley Dean Witter, October 10, 2000.

Herath, Hemantha S. B., and Chan S. Park. "Economic Analysis of R&D Projects: An Options Approach," *The Engineering Economist*, 44, No. 1, 1999, pp. 1–35.

Kaplan, Robert, S., and David P. Norton. *The Balanced Scorecard* (Boston: Harvard Business School Press, 1996).

———. "Having Trouble With Your Strategy? Then Map It," *Harvard Business Review OnPoint*, Number 5165, 2000.

Krell, Eric. "Finance/Accounting Software," *Business Finance*, August 2001.

Leahy, Tad. "The Holy Grail of Shareholder Value Measurement," *Business Finance*, February 2000.

McNulty, James J., Tony D. Yeh, William S. Schulze, and Michael Lubatkin. "What Is Your Real Cost of Capital?" *Harvard Business Review*, October 2000, pp. 114–121.

Nohria, Nitin, William Joyce, and Bruce Roberson. "What Really Works," *Harvard Business Review OnPoint*, No. 4260, July 2003.

Project Management Institute. *A Guide to the Project Management Body of Knowledge* (Newtown Square, PA: Author, 2000).

Rappaport, Alfred, and Michael J. Mauboussin. *Expectations Investing: Reading Stock Prices for Better Returns* (Boston: Harvard Business School Press, 2001).

Rizzuto, Janis. "The Case for Earned Value," *ProjectsAtWork*, July–August 2003, pp. 31–32.

Roach, Stephen S. "Capital Spending Myths," *Global: Daily Economic Comment*, Morgan Stanley Equity Research, March 5, 2003.

Schoenberger, Chana R. "Consider Your Options," *Forbes*, December 25, 2000, p. 276.

Serven, Lawrence. "Passing the ROI Test: A Three-Tier Model of Obtaining Project Funding," *Business Performance Management*, June 2003, pp. 14–19.

Slywotzky, Adrian, J., David J. Morrison, and Karl Webber. *How Digital Is Your Business?* (New York: Crown Business, 2000).

Stein, Jeremy C. "Rational Capital Budgeting in an Irrational World," *Journal of Business,* 69, 1996, pp. 429–455.

Swisher, Kara, with Lisa Dickey. *There Must Be a Pony in Here Somewhere: The AOL Time Warner Debacle and the Quest for the Digital Future* (New York: Crown Business, 2003).

Web Sites

www.adnet.com

www.broadcastingcable.com

www.cfo.com

INDEX